GOD'S LOVE for God's Children

STORY DEVOTIONS FOR FAMILY TIME

ELDON WEISHEIT

AUGSBURG Publishing House • Minneapolis

GOD'S LOVE FOR GOD'S CHILDREN
Story Devotions for Family Time

Library of Congress Cataloging-in-Publication Data

Weisheit, Eldon.
GOD'S LOVE FOR GOD'S CHILDREN.

   1. Family—Prayer-books and devotions—English.
I. Title.
BV255.W45   1986   249   86-3397
ISBN 0-8066-2213-X

Manufactured in the U.S.A.   APH 10-2680

1   2   3   4   5   6   7   8   9   0   1   2   3   4   5   6   7   8   9

To the staff and students of
Fountain of Life Lutheran School and Daycare
for sharing their stories and their lives with me

Contents

A Word to Parents and Teachers

Parents and teachers like to tell stories about children. I am a parent, and as a pastor I spend a lot of time teaching children. As you read these stories, you will easily see that I enjoyed writing them.

But I didn't write—and I hope you don't read—these stories only for entertainment. Each story is to help children and the significant adults in their lives to recognize themselves. The stories are to help their readers and hearers say or feel, "That happened to me," or "I felt that way too."

The stories are intended to help you in several ways as you relate to the children in your life.

First, they are conversation starters. Parents and teachers often have important subjects to discuss with children. But sometimes it's hard to work the subject into a conversation. If you bring up the topic, especially if it's a moral issue, it becomes a monolog in which you speak and the children listen—you hope. But a story gives the children a chance to get involved. They can identify with one of the people in the story, or they can disagree with someone in the story. They can say what they would have done or said, and you can do the same.

These stories will also help you and your children know that certain problems are common among us. Each of us often thinks we are alone in certain situations. A story in a book lets you

9

and the children in your life know that others have thought and done the same things.

You and your children may not have faced some of the issues presented in this book. Many children have no brothers or sisters, many have not experienced divorce in their families, a few may live in areas where there is usually no need to be afraid of strangers. Yet hearing about things that happen to others helps children be prepared for future events in their own lives and also helps them understand what is happening to others. Just as it is good for the child from a two-parent family to read about a single-parent family, the child with one parent needs to hear stories about those who live with a mother and father.

A few suggestions

Older children may wish to read the stories on their own. Let them decide if they want to discuss their reading with you. You might ask an older child to suggest which of the stories you should read. Just as you have an agenda of things you want to tell your children, they have a list of things that they think you should know.

Make reading the stories to younger children a special event. Let it be a family time together with the TV off and members of the family sitting close together. Sometimes it is good for story time to be a quiet time between one parent and one child. In any case, it needs to be regular, so that children can grow in security and become aware that it is a time for conversation.

Each story ends with some questions. Don't feel compelled to use every question, and add other questions that are important for your family. Remember, the questions are not tests to see if the children listened. Instead they are a way to get the conversation started and keep it going.

Include the Bible readings from a translation that the children can understand. And let them participate in reading the scripture passages.

A prayer is included at the end of each devotion and some extra prayers are found at the end of this book. These prayers are "starters." Include simple prayers of your own and encourage the children to do the same.

These stories will give you many opportunities to let your children know that you believe in Jesus. Sharing your faith with children gives them a security that will last an eternity. Talking about Jesus lets them know he is a part of the events in their lives and that he is with us because he wants to be.

Good Morning, God!
Psalm 118:24, 28-29

"Good morning, Laurie!" her mother said as Laurie came into the kitchen and sat down for breakfast.

Laurie didn't answer. She drank some milk and looked at the cereal box.

"I said 'Good morning,' " her mother repeated. "Did you hear me?"

"I heard you," said Laurie, "but I'm tired and don't feel like talking yet."

"I know that when you first get up, you don't like to talk," said her mother. "But I'd like to help you start out the day in a happy way. If you start out being grouchy and grumpy, you can make everyone else unhappy too."

"But I don't feel happy in the morning," said Laurie.

"That's too bad, and I'd like to help you," said her mother. "Your daddy helps me start out the day in a good way, and I help him. We each say 'Good morning' to each other."

"But what if you don't think it is a good morning?"

"Saying 'Good morning' to each other doesn't mean it is a good morning," explained her mother. "It means, 'I hope you have a good morning.' When I said 'Good morning' to you a little while ago, I was trying to give you a happy day. I wanted you to give me a happy day too."

"OK," said Laurie. "Good morning!"

"Thank you!" said her mother. "There's something else I do. I say 'Good morning' to God each day."

"But you don't have to tell God to have a good day," said Laurie. "God can always have a good day."

"Yes, he can," said her mother. "But God wants to share his good day with us. Every morning I remember that God loves me. I think that is his way of saying good morning to me. So I say the same thing back to him."

"OK," said Laurie. "Good morning, God!"

"Now we've all said hello to each other," said her mother. "Let's eat breakfast!"

Some questions

Are you happy or grouchy when you get up in the morning? Are the other members of your family happy in the morning? How could you help make each other happy?

A prayer

Dear God, please be with me each morning when I wake up, and help me to get a good start every day. In Jesus' name. Amen.

Let's Play a Game!
1 Timothy 4:12

"Come on, Dad, let's play a game," said Billy as the family finished eating dinner.

"What do you want to play?" asked his father.

"Let's play checkers," answered Billy, "because I beat you the last time."

"But I won the two times before that," said his father.

"Then I'll win this time and we'll be even," said Billy as he got out the checkerboard.

"I like to win when I play any game," said Billy. "Do you like to win?"

"Yes, I like to win," said his father. "But I like to see you win too."

"Do you play to let me win?" asked Billy.

"No," answered his father. "If you win when we play, it's because you played well."

"Then why did you say you like to see me win?" Billy asked. "Don't you want to win all the time?"

"Now you understand why I like to play with you," explained his father. "I like to win when I play. Because you're my son and I love you, I also like to see you win. So when I play with you, I can be happy if I win, and I can be happy if you win."

"But I want to win every time I play with you," said Billy.

"Sure you do!" said his father. "You like to wrestle with me to see if you can sit on me. You like to see how you are growing, and you want to be bigger than me."

"How did you know that?" asked Billy.

"Because that's how I felt about my dad when I was growing up," said his father. "Children always want to do as well as or better than their parents."

"Don't parents want to do better than their kids?" asked Billy.

"No, we like to see you do better than we did," said his father. "Your mother and I want you to be happy. You don't have to prove to us how great you are; we already know that. But we're always happy when you do things that make you happy."

"OK, I'll be happy when I beat you," said Billy. "It's your move."

Some questions

Can you enjoy a game even if you lose?

Do you like to compete with your parents? With your brothers and sisters?

Can you win without making those who lose feel bad?

A prayer

Dear Jesus, be with me when I play games. Help me enjoy the game and help those who play with me enjoy the game too. Amen.

They Say I'm Stupid
Psalm 102:8

Carlos didn't go in the house when he came home from school. Instead, he went to the backyard where his teenage brother Jess was working on his car.

"Hi, kid!" said Jess. "How's it going?"

"Terrible!" said Carlos.

"Hey, what's the matter with you?" his big brother asked.

"The kids at school don't like me," said Carlos. "They say I'm stupid."

"You're not stupid," said Jess. "Who said that?"

"I don't know their names," said Carlos. "They're in the fourth or fifth grade. But they walk home the same way I do, and they pick on me."

"Do you know why they pick on you?" asked Jess.

"Because they don't like me," said Carlos, "and they think I'm stupid."

"They don't even know you," said Jess. "Your teacher, the other kids in your class, and your family know you're not stupid. We like you."

"Then why do they pick on me?" asked Carlos.

"Because you're littler than they are, and they want to think they're big shots," said Jess. "When big kids pick on one little kid it shows what kind of people they are. It doesn't say anything against you. They're the ones who look bad."

"That doesn't help me at all," said Carlos. "Yesterday they took my books away and threw them over the fence. I had to climb the fence to get them."

"Look, little brother," said Jess. "I'm not very old yet but I've learned a few things. Anyone who has fun by trying to make other people feel bad has problems. Don't ever be like those guys. Are you nice to kids who are littler than you?"

"Sure I am!" said Carlos. "I wouldn't do what those guys do to me."

"That's good!" said Jess. "Tell you what—tomorrow I'll walk home from school with you. How's that?"

"Would you really?" said Carlos. "Thanks a lot!"

Some questions

Do you know anyone who is a bully? Do you think anyone else thinks you are a bully?

If you call someone else bad names does it make the other person look bad? Or does it make you sound bad?

Can you still feel good about yourself when someone calls you bad names? Why?

16

A prayer

Lord Jesus, I'm glad you love me. Help me to love and to live with people who don't know how to give love. Amen.

The Rest of the Story
Luke 7:11-16

"Why are you two back so soon?" Mrs. Burris asked her two children as they came in the back door.

"We wanted to get here before old Mrs. Green phoned you," said Miriam.

"Why is Mrs. Green going to call me?" asked their mother.

"Because she says we were playing in the alley," said Tommy. "We were not playing in the alley. We were in our yard. The ball went in the alley. I looked both ways, Mom, honest I did! I was very careful before I went to get it. But she's a grouchy old lady. She yelled at me and said she was going to call you."

"She yelled at me, too," said Miriam. "I didn't even go in the alley, but she said I was too close. We can't have any fun with her living next door."

"Every time we go in the backyard she watches us," said Tommy. "She wants to get us into trouble."

"Mrs. Green hasn't phoned me, and I don't think she will," their mother said. "You've told me your story, and I believe you. But maybe I should tell you the rest of the story."

"We told you everything, Mom," said Tommy. "Honest!"

"You told me everything that happened today," said Mrs. Burris. "But part of the story happened almost 20 years ago."

"We weren't here then," said Miriam, "so we can't be blamed for what happened 20 years ago."

"This part of the story did not involve you," said their mother. "But I want you to hear it, so you can understand Mrs. Green. You know that Mr. and Mrs. Green do not have any children."

"And I'm glad," said Tommy. "They're mean to kids."

"But they did have a little boy once. They loved him very much. One day when he was about five years old, he was riding his skateboard in the alley when the garbage truck came along. The driver did not see him and ran over him. Mr. and Mrs. Green's little boy was killed."

Tommy and Miriam sat very still for a long time.

"You mean he was killed right out there?" asked Tommy.

"No," their mother said. "They lived in a different house then. They moved here because they did not like to see the place where their little boy was killed."

"Do you think that when she sees us in the alley, or even close to it, she thinks about her little boy?" asked Miriam.

"Yes," said her mother. "That's the rest of the story."

"Maybe we could play beside the house instead of back there," said Miriam. "Does Mrs. Green want us to play where she never sees us at all?"

"No. She loves you, and it helps her to see you," said their mother. "She likes you so much she never wants you to be hurt."

"She might even let us play in her yard," said Tommy. "Let's go and ask her."

Some questions

Have people been angry at you because they knew about something you had done but did not know the rest of the story?

Could you have been angry at someone because you did not know the rest of the story?

Name some ways you could find out the rest of the story about other people.

A prayer

Dear God, help me not to find fault with others, and help others not to find fault with me. In Jesus' name. Amen.

He's a Pest!
Psalm 133

"Mom!" Jess yelled, "Will you make Carlos stay out of my room? He's a pest!"

"What did Carlos do?" asked his mother.

"What he always does," said Jess. "I was listening to music on my headphones and he pulled out the plug."

"Don't you see that he wants attention from you?" asked his mother. "Carlos is a little boy. He thinks its great to have a big brother who is a teenager. He wants to be around you."

"Why does he pick on me all the time?" asked Jess. "He's a royal pest."

"He's only trying to get your attention," said his mother.

The next evening, Jess was lying on his bed with his headphones on. His eyes were closed. All of a sudden the music stopped. Jess saw Carlos drop the plug and run. Jess jumped from the bed and grabbed his little brother's leg as he headed for the door.

"Mom! Mom!" yelled Carlos. "Jess is going to hit me!" But to Carlos's surprise his big brother did not hit him. Instead, Jess lay down on the floor and let Carlos sit on top of him.

"Want to wrestle?" asked Jess.

"Sure!" said his younger brother.

The two boys played on the floor. They tickled each other, laughed, and yelled.

"Hey, let me go!" said Carlos. "There's something I want to see on TV."

"OK," said Jess as he plugged the headphones back in, put them on, and lay down on the bed. As he listened to the music, he smiled. Having a little brother could be fun—once you knew how to put up with him.

Some questions

Do you know how to get others to pay attention to you when you need them?

Can you think of anyone who is trying to get your attention?

Dear God, help me understand other people, and help them understand me. In Jesus' name. Amen.

What Do You Want to Talk About?

1 John 3:1-3

"Have you ever been in my office before, Lisa?" the pastor asked as they entered the room.

"No," said Lisa, and the look on her faced showed she was not eager to be in his office even then.

"Lots of people come to talk to me here," said the pastor. "I'm glad you came to see me today. Your mother and father thought that we should have a talk."

"OK," said Lisa as she sat down.

"What would you like to talk about?" asked the pastor.

"My report card," said Lisa. "Do you know what kind of grades I got?"

"If you want to talk about them, I know you got good grades," said the pastor. "How many 'A's?"

"All but one," said Lisa. "That was in spelling. I can't remember if it is i-before-e or e-before-i."

"I'm glad you do well in school, and I like to talk to you about that," said the pastor. "Is there anything else you'd like to talk about?"

"Do you know I have a cat?" said Lisa. "His name is King Arthur. He always sits on the best chair in our living room like it's his throne."

"I've met King Arthur," said the pastor. "He's a pretty cat. Is there something you *don't* want to talk about?"

"The divorce," murmured Lisa.

"Do you think we should talk about grades and pets or about the divorce?" asked the pastor.

"The divorce," said Lisa.

"That's what your parents wanted us to talk about," said the pastor. "Do you know that both of them have been coming to my office too?"

"Yes," said Lisa.

"They want you to know that they tried to stay together," said the pastor. "Both of them have made some mistakes. They don't want their mistakes to hurt you."

"Will I get to be with both of them?" asked Lisa.

"Yes," said the pastor. "You still have a mother, and you still have a father. They've learned two lessons from their divorce. They didn't talk to each other like they should have. And they didn't know they could talk to someone else about their problems."

"They argued all the time," said Lisa.

"Yes, they argued instead of talking," said the pastor. "That's why they wanted you to talk to me. They want you to know that you can talk to someone about problems—even about things you don't want to talk about. If you learn that when you are young it will help you when you grow up."

"I'm glad I can talk to you," said Lisa.

Some questions

What are some things you like to talk about?

What are some things you don't want to talk about?

Whom could you talk to about the things you like to talk about? About the things you don't like to talk about?

A prayer

Lord Jesus, I like talking to you. Help me be able to talk to others also. Amen.

What Do You Think?

2 Timothy 2:1

Megan was worried. Her teacher had asked her to pin up pictures on the board. The class was studying airplanes. Mr. Reich had given her a box full of plane pictures. She knew she could not put all the pictures on the board. She did not know what to do with all of them.

"Oh, I forgot to give you these," said Mr. Reich as he handed Megan a box of thumbtacks. "You'll need them to put up the pictures."

"Which pictures do you want me to put on the board?" asked Megan.

"Pick the ones you think look nice and that will help us learn more about planes," answered Mr. Reich.

Megan looked through the pictures. She wondered which ones Mr. Reich really wanted her to use.

"Do you need anything else?" asked Mr. Reich as he came back once more.

"No," said Megan. "Do you want me to use this picture?"

"Use the picture you like," said the teacher.

"But I don't know which pictures you want me to like," said Megan.

Mr. Reich sat down beside her. "It's not important which pictures I like," he said. "Pick the ones you like. Your opinion is worthwhile."

"But I'm doing this for you," she said.

"No, I asked you to do it because I know you can," said Mr. Reich. "You know as much about airplanes as anyone else in the class. You can make the board look nice and be interesting."

"Do you think this picture would be a good one to use?" asked Megan.

"What do you think?" asked Mr. Reich.

"I don't think I'll use it," said Megan. "I like this one better."

"Then use that one," said Mr. Reich.

Is your opinion important to some people?
What decisions do you make for yourself?
Do you want someone to help you with some decisions?

A prayer

Lord, help me decide what I can and what I cannot do. Amen.

I Don't Think I Can
1 Corinthians 12:4-7

All the students in Miss Aldridge's second grade were busy. They were getting ready for a special music program. First they would give the program in the gym for the other students. Then they would invite all the parents to see them on a Friday night.

"Randy, I have something very special I want you to do," said Miss Aldridge as she sat down beside him.

"What?" he asked.

"I want you to sing a song for our program," she said.

"I don't think I can," said Randy.

"I heard you singing when we were doing the song for the entire class," said the teacher. "You have a good voice."

"But I don't want to sing by myself," said Randy.

"If you don't want to, you don't have to," said Miss Aldridge. "But I'd like you to think about it."

"I don't like to stand up in front of people," said Randy.

"But you like to sing," said the teacher.

"But I don't know if I can do it right," said Randy.

"You may make a mistake," said Miss Aldridge. "We all make mistakes sometimes. The mistakes we make don't wipe out the good things we do. You can sing well."

"Someone might laugh at me," he said.

"And many people might clap for you," said the teacher. "Remember, I asked you to sing. That means I think you can

23

do it better than anyone else in the class. If I didn't think that, I would not have asked you."

Randy sat still for a long time. He had always been afraid to do anything in front of people. He wanted to say "No!" with a very loud voice. But instead he heard himself saying, "OK, I'll try."

At first he was sorry he said it. But when he saw the happy smile on Miss Aldridge's face, he felt better. She knew a lot about singing; maybe he *could* sing.

Some questions

Are you afraid to do things because you might make a mistake?

Do you have to be perfect in everything you do? Why not?

Do you like other people even if they make mistakes?

A prayer

Dear God, help me do the things that you have given me the ability to do. In Jesus' name. Amen.

Broken Truth
Proverbs 23:22-25

As soon as dinner was over, Lance ran to the telephone to call his friend Eric. He and Eric had just come back from a three-day camping trip with a group of boys from church.

"Hi!" Lance said when his friend answered the phone. "It was fun to eat at home again, right?"

"Yeah," said his friend, "but I had gotten used to sand in my food. I sort of missed it."

The boys laughed at the things they had done and talked about some of the other boys they had met.

"Why did you tell all those guys that your dad was a doctor?" asked Eric. "I thought he was a salesman."

"But he sells things to hospitals, so it's all the same thing," said Lance.

"It's not the same thing to me," said Eric. "I heard you say a lot of things that weren't true."

"Like what?" asked Lance.

"You said you lived in a great big house with a swimming pool," said Eric.

"Our house is big enough," said Lance, "and we have a wading pool that we put up every summer."

"And you said you were the pitcher on our ball team," said Eric. "I've never seen you pitch."

"I did at practice one time," said Lance.

"I think you told a lot of lies," said Eric.

"I didn't lie," said Lance. "I just stretched the truth a little."

"My dad says that when you stretch the truth it breaks," said Eric. "And when you break the truth it's a lie."

"I didn't hurt anyone," said Lance.

"I like you better when you act normal," said Eric. "You kept trying to be a big shot."

"I was just having some fun," said Lance.

"But it's more fun to be real," said Eric. "I know what your dad does and what kind of house you live in, and I know you aren't very good at baseball. But you're my friend; you don't have to pretend to be something special. Besides that, we are Jesus' friends, and that makes us special. We don't have to try to be something more than we really are."

Lance was quiet for a while. "I'm glad you are my friend," he said. "I guess I forgot that while we were camping."

Some questions

Why do some people have to brag to make themselves sound important?

Do you feel more important if you stretch the truth?

What do you think when you hear someone else bragging?

A prayer

Jesus, help me understand who I am and what I can do, so that I can be honest about myself. Amen.

May I Watch TV?
1 Peter 1:13-15

"May I watch TV?" Cindy asked her mother.

"What are you going to watch?" her mother asked.

"I don't know," said Cindy. "I'll find something."

"That's not the way to use television," said her mother. "You shouldn't turn it on just to see what's there; you should turn it on to see a program that you want to watch."

"I don't care what's on!" said Cindy. "I'm just bored and don't have anything to do."

"I'm sorry that I'm busy now and can't spend time with you," said her mother. "I've got to get dinner ready."

"Then let me watch TV," said Cindy.

"No," said her mother. "The TV is not a babysitter. Get the TV schedule and I'll check to see if there is anything on now for you to watch."

"Why do you care about what I watch?" asked Cindy. "I won't watch any bad shows that you don't like."

"I just don't want you to get in the habit of using TV as something to do," said her mother.

"TV isn't bad," said Cindy.

"No, TV isn't bad," said her mother. "In fact, TV is a good thing, but we must use it the right way."

"What's the right way?" asked Cindy.

"You can watch programs that you will enjoy, or those that teach you something," said her mother. "But don't use the TV to fill the time when you have nothing else to do."

"Why not?" asked Cindy.

"God has given you many worthwhile things to do. That's why you should learn to do things that help you or someone else," said her mother. "If you read a book, you are doing something—not just watching. If you go and play outside, you are getting exercise and enjoying flowers and the outdoors."

"What else could I do?" asked Cindy.
"You could help me cook our dinner," said her mother.
"I think I'd like to read a book," said Cindy.

Some questions

How many hours a day do you watch TV?
What are some good things you could do instead of watching TV?
How does Jesus help us spend our time in a good way?

A prayer

Dear God, thank you for TV. Help me use it the right way, and help me also do other interesting things. In Jesus' name. Amen.

I Don't Love You
1 John 4:19-21

"Peter," his father said, "I told you to be home at 5:00 this afternoon, and you didn't get home until after 5:30. Why were you late?"
"We were playing at Brian's house and I forgot," said Peter.
"I asked Brian's mother to tell you to come home at a quarter to five. Did she?" his father asked.
"Yes, she told me," said Peter. "But the other kids didn't have to go home then, so I stayed too."
"I don't care what time the others go home," said his father. "Each family has their own rules. You were to be home by five. That means you are grounded for one week. You can't play with your friends all next week and not on Saturday either."
"But we have lots of plans for next week," protested Peter.
"I'm sorry," said his father, "but you must learn to come home when you are told to."
"I don't love you anymore," said Peter.
"I still love you, son," said his father.

"No, you don't!" said Peter. "If you loved me, you would let me play with my friends."

"I look at it this way," said his father. "Because I love you, I will correct you if you do something wrong."

"If you think I did something wrong, then you can't love me," said Peter.

"I can love you even when you have been wrong," said his father.

"I don't love you when you hurt me," said Peter. "How can you love me if you think I did something wrong?"

"Because that's what love is all about," said his father. "We can give each other the kind of love that God gives us. God loves us even when we do something wrong. God sent Jesus to be our Savior and to forgive our sins. Because God still loves me, I can still love you."

"But you can't love me if I don't love you," said Peter.

"Yes I can," said his father. "And if I love you, then you can love me too."

"I don't think it will work," said Peter.

"That's how God does it," said his father, "and it works."

Some questions

Will God love you even if you don't love God?

Did you love *God* first, or did God love *you* first?

Can you be angry at someone and still love that person?

A prayer

Thank you, Jesus, for loving me even when I don't love you and others as I should. Give me your love so I can love you and others. Amen.

When I Was Born
Psalm 8

Janice and Andy were helping their mother clean out the drawers in her dresser. They liked to see all the things their mother kept.

"Did you see this?" asked their mother. "This is the birth announcement we sent out when Andy was born."

"Let me see," said Andy. "What does it say?"

"It says your name is really Andrew Alan," said Janice.

"And it says you weighed eight pounds and four ounces," said their mother. "You were 21 inches long."

"Do you remember when I was born?" Andy asked his sister.

"Yes," she said. "You were little and funny-looking and you cried a lot."

"Did I?" Andy asked his mother.

"You were a darling little baby, and we all were glad to have you in our family," said his mother. "Look, Janice, here is your birth announcement."

"Let me see," said Janice. "It says I was 19 inches long and weighed eight pounds and six ounces."

"What is the rest of your name?" asked Andy.

"Janice Ellen," she answered without looking. "What did I look like when I was a baby?" she asked her mother.

"You were very pretty," said her mother. "You had lots of black hair and you always kept your eyes closed."

"Did I cry a lot?" she asked.

"You cried a little," said her mother. "But babies are supposed to cry. You were a good baby. Your father and I would take turns holding you."

"Did you hold me when I was born?" asked Andy.

"Sure we did!" his mother answered. "Haven't you noticed? We still like to hold both of you."

"Like right now!" said Janice as she joined her brother on her mother's lap.

"Yes, like right now," answered their mother, as she gave each child a kiss. "But we have work to do."

"That's right," said Janice, "we're supposed to help you. Come on, Andrew Alan, let's get to work!"

Some questions

What do you know about your birth and about yourself as a little baby?

Who else, besides our parents, loves us and wants to hold us close?

Would you like to know more about yourself as a little baby?

A prayer

Heavenly Father, thank you for letting me be born and thank you also for all the others in my family. In Jesus' name. Amen.

I'm All Alone
Ecclesiastes 4:9-12

Nicole felt sorry for herself. When she came home from school, her mother was asleep. Her mother had a night job, so she had to take a nap in the afternoon. Nicole always had to come home very quietly. She could not bring friends with her because they would make noise and awaken her mother.

"I'm always by myself," Nicole said to herself. "When Daddy comes home, he is always too tired to play with me. He has to have his dinner and rest. Then I have to go to bed."

Nicole crawled up on the top bunk of her bed with a big teddy bear. She hugged the bear.

"At least you have time to be with me," she said to the bear. "You don't have to go to work, and you don't get tired. But you don't talk, either. And you can't play any games with me."

Nicole remembered going home with her friend Maria one day after school. Maria had a big family. Her mother was at home, and her grandmother lived with the family. Nicole liked all the noise and fun at Maria's house.

"I wish I could live with Maria," she said to the bear. "Then I wouldn't be alone all the time."

Nicole remembered the Saturday Maria came to her house. She thought about what Maria had said: "You have a bedroom all by yourself. I have to share a room with my little sister and my grandmother. I wish I could have a room by myself."

Nicole looked around her room. She wished she had a grandmother with her right now. A little sister would be even better.

Then Nicole remembered how Maria thought it was strange that she had two beds. "You mean," Maria had said, "you have a lower bunk to sleep in, and one up there to play in?"

For the first time since she came home, Nicole smiled. "Isn't that funny?" she said to herself. "I wish I were at Maria's house, because it is full of people and noisy. Right now Maria may be wishing she were here because it's quiet and I'm alone."

"But I don't feel sorry for Maria," Nicole told her bear. "And I guess she doesn't feel sorry for me, either."

Some questions

Do the people in your family need to spend more time together? How could you be together more?

Would you rather live the way someone else does? Why?

Do you think someone else might like to live the way you do? Why?

A prayer

Dear Jesus, help me to enjoy what I have and not feel sorry for myself. Amen.

They'll Be Sorry for What They Did

Luke 15:11-32

Mark was angry. No, he was more than angry; he was mad—very mad. His mother and father had sent him to his room. It was Saturday, the one day he had to play. Now he had to spend the whole afternoon in one room. And he didn't even have a TV in his room like his friend Jimmy did.

"They don't really love me," Mark said to himself as he thought about his parents. "They don't want me to have any fun."

Mark looked at the window. He knew he could sneak out the window and go over to Jimmy's house and watch TV.

"They'll be sorry for what they did when they come to call me for dinner and I'm not here," he said to himself. "They'll think I'm dead or that someone kidnapped me. Then they'll be sorry!"

Mark quickly crawled out the window and ran down the alley. No one saw him go. He ran to Jimmy's house, but no one was home. Then he remembered that Jimmy's family had gone to visit his grandmother for the weekend.

Mark walked down to the shopping center. His mother and father would never let him go there by himself. He found a store that had a big fish tank. He liked to watch the fish. He wondered if his mother knew he was gone yet.

"She'll be sorry when she finds out I'm not there," he said to himself. He thought about how his mother would call his father and how they would look all over the house and yard. Then they'd call Jimmy's house, but no one would answer.

As Mark watched the fish, he kept thinking about his mother. She would be crying. His father would get in the car and drive around the neighborhood. He might cry too. Would they call the police? Would they think he was hurt and go to the hospital to look for him?

"If they do all those things, they must love me," Mark

thought to himself. "If they love me, why did they make me spend the whole afternoon in my room?" Mark thought about the things he had said to his mother. They were not good things. He did not mean them. She should have known that.

Suddenly Mark ran out of the store toward home. He was glad he had left the window open so that he could crawl back into his room. He could hear his mother and father talking in the kitchen. He was glad they did not know he had been away.

Some questions

Do you know anyone who has run away from home? What happened to the family?

If you hurt someone in your family while you are angry, whom else are you hurting? Will that cause more problems?

Who still loves us when we do things that are wrong?

A prayer

Lord Jesus, thank you for loving me even when I do something wrong. Help me to love others even when I think they have done something wrong. Amen.

We're Having Company!
Psalm 100

"Are we having company tonight?" asked Crystal when she came in the house and saw the dining room table set with all the special dishes.

"Yes," said her mother. "Find your sister and tell her it's time to get ready for dinner."

Crystal found Lori, and they both ran to the bathroom to comb their hair and freshen up. When they came back, they saw their father come in from the backyard where he had been cooking on the grill.

"How come there are only four places at the table?" asked Lori. "Don't we get to eat with you?"

"Sure you do," said her father. "You sit right there, Lori. Crystal can sit opposite you."

"But where will you and Mommy sit?" asked Lori.

"I'll sit at this place," said her father, "and your mother will sit there."

"But where is the company going to sit?" asked Crystal.

"You are the company," said their mother. "This is a special dinner for some special guests. And you are the guests."

"You mean you got out the nice dishes just for us?" asked Lori.

"And Daddy cooked outside on the grill just for us?" asked Crystal.

"Yes," said their father. "We think you are the best company we can have, so we are having a fancy dinner for you."

"Wow!" said Crystal. "I can't wait to tell my friends about our special dinner."

"Can't we do this every night?" asked Lori.

"No," her mother said. "This is something special for just once in a while. We want you to know how important you are to us."

"Come on, let's eat," their father said.

Some questions

When is the best time for your family to be together?
Do you let the others in your family know that you like them?
How do others in your family show that they like you?

A prayer

Come, Lord Jesus, eat with us. Bless the food we eat and help us to love one another. Amen.

I Didn't Do It
Luke 12:57-59

"Greg, we've got a problem that we have to talk about," his father said to him.

"What's wrong now?" asked Greg.

"Mrs. Ellis phoned me last night," his father said. "Were you playing in her yard again?"

"Just for a little bit," said Greg. "We were running away from some kids from the other school, so we hid in her yard."

"She has told you before, and I have told you, not to play in her yard," said his father. "But this time we have a more serious problem."

"What?" asked Greg.

"Some of her flowers were trampled down," said his father, "and her birdbath was knocked over and broken."

"I didn't do it," said Greg.

"Mrs. Ellis didn't say you did it," said his father. "But her birdbath was in good shape yesterday morning. She saw you in her yard. Now it is broken. That looks bad for you."

"But I didn't do it!" said Greg. "Maybe the kids from the other school came looking for us and broke it."

"Maybe so," said his father. "But Mrs. Ellis didn't see anyone else in her yard; she saw you."

"That's not fair!" said Greg. "She should have watched to see who did it."

"No, son, she should not have to watch her own backyard," said his father. "You should not have been on her property. She has asked you before not to play in her yard. I told you not to go there."

"I'm sorry," said Greg. "We were running from those guys."

"You should have run somewhere else," said his father. "Now we are going to go see Mrs. Ellis. You will have to work for her to pay for the birdbath."

"But I told you I didn't break it," said Greg.

"You may have been running and bumped it without even knowing it," said his father. "You can ask your friends to help you pay for it, if you think they did it. But you must learn not to go on other people's property."

"OK," said Greg. "Let me phone Bobby. He was there too."

Do you think Greg should pay for the birdbath? Should Mrs. Ellis have to pay for it?

If you are in a place where you should not be, could you get blamed for doing something you did not do?

A prayer

Dear God, help me to think about other people and not to do anything to hurt them. In Jesus' name. Amen.

You Won't Let Me Have Any Fun
John 10:1-6

"Daddy! Daddy!" Joel yelled as he ran into the house. "Kirk has a new motorbike, and he said I can go for a ride with him if you say it is OK. May I go? Please!"

"Slow down a little, son," said his father. "You must be as excited as Kirk is about his motorbike."

"It's neat!" said Joel. "Can I ride with Kirk?"

"No," said his father. "That was nice of Kirk to invite you for a ride, but riding on a motorbike can be dangerous."

"Kirk is a good driver," said Joel. "He's 17 years old and he has his license to drive. You said he was a good kid."

"Yes, Kirk is a good kid," said his father. "In fact, I suppose we had better start thinking of him as a young man. You know we like him and his family. I'm glad he is so good to you."

"Then you'll let me ride with him?" asked Joel.

"No," said his father. "I trust Kirk, but riding a motorbike can be dangerous even for good drivers. And having an extra person on the back makes it even more dangerous."

"But I know he'll be careful," said Joel.

"Yes, but if the other driver makes a mistake, it is the person on the bike who gets hurt," said his father.

"You won't ever let me have any fun," said Joel.

"I want you to have fun," said his father. "But I don't want you to get hurt."

"How do you know I'll get hurt if I ride with Kirk?"

"I didn't say I knew you'd get hurt," said his father. "I just know that riding a motorbike can be dangerous. Not everyone who rides one gets hurt, but many do. I don't want you to take the risk."

"Can I ride with him after he has had the bike for a while and becomes a very good driver?" asked Joel.

"Let's discuss that later," said his father. "For now, I've told you that you cannot ride the bike. I'm supposed to take care of you, and you'll have to accept my decision."

Some questions

Is it true that Joel's father did not want him to have fun or that he did not want Joel to get hurt?

Why do children need to ask their parents' permission to do some things?

Should parents sometimes say no to their children?

A prayer

Dear God, thank you for my parents and those who teach me what to do. Help me to listen to them and to help them listen to me. In Jesus' name. Amen.

Something That Will Last
Luke 6:46-49

John was sad. He and his father had worked very hard to make a kite. His whole family agreed that it was the best kite they had ever seen. The first time that John flew the kite, the string broke. The kite landed on some high power lines. The wind tossed the kite around and it broke.

"Look at all the work we did," John said to his father. "And I lost the kite the first time I used it. We wasted all our time."

"No, we didn't," said his father. "We had fun making the kite. I liked being with you, and I know you liked being with me. We have good memories. We also learned a lot about making kites. We can make another one sometime. You will know how to make one for your children someday."

"But I wanted that kite," said John.

"I understand, son," said his father. "But maybe that kite has taught you an important lesson."

"You mean how to make kites?" asked John.

"No, more important than that!" said his father. "Learn to be happy about things that will last a long time. If you are happy only because you have a kite, your happiness won't last long. Sooner or later, kites break or get lost. Most of the things we have are temporary; we keep them only a short time. But some things will last a long time."

"Like what?" asked John.

"Like the things you learn," said his father. "You are learning to read and write and do other things. What you learn will last as long as you live."

"That's a long time," said John.

"Some things will last even longer than that," said his father. "You know that Jesus loves you and is with you. You don't have to worry about his love going away. It will last even longer than you live. Even when you die, Jesus will still love you, and he will bring you back to life again."

"Do you think it's wrong for me to be sad about my kite?"

"No, I understand," said his father. "I just want you to know that you've got more to be happy about than a kite. When you think about what you lost, I hope you also will remember what you still have."

Some questions

What's the most important thing you have right now?
How long will it last?
What do you have that will last the longest?

A prayer

Thank you, Jesus, for loving me. Thanks for all the other things I have, too. Help me remember what the most important part of my life is. Amen.

Dad Said I Could!
Matthew 21:28-32

"Mom, may I go over to play at Leslie's this afternoon?" asked Sandy after she had eaten lunch on Saturday.

"No, not today," her mother answered.

"But Dad said I could," Sandy answered.

"I told you that you can't go," said mother.

"Dad told me I could go," said Sandy. "You can call him and ask him."

"I don't have to call and ask him," said her mother. "As far as he was concerned, you could go. But as far as I am concerned, you cannot go!"

"But that's not fair!" said Sandy.

"You may think it's not fair," said her mother. "Your father did not know that you didn't clean your room this morning and that you have to clean it this afternoon. He also does not know that you and Leslie got into trouble the last time you spent the afternoon at her house."

"When Dad gets home, I'm going to tell him you wouldn't let me go even though he said I could," said Sandy.

"I think that is a good idea," said her mother. "You have tried to play your father against me, and me against him, several times. We have talked about it, and we agreed not to let you do that."

"Do what?" asked Sandy.

"You ask one of us something as a way to make the other one go along with what you want," said her mother. "You asked me if you could watch TV the other night. I said yes because I did not know that your father had told you to do your homework. You tried to tell him you didn't have to do the homework because I said you could watch TV."

"I guess I can't go to see Sara then, either?" asked Sandy.

"No," said her mother, "but you can go and see that your room is cleaned up. Then you and I will bake some cakes."

Some questions

Do you ever try to play one parent against another like Sandy did?

Why will one parent sometimes say yes while the other will say no to the same request?

A prayer

Thank you, God, for my parents. Help me listen to both of them, and help them. And help them listen to me and help me. In Jesus' name. Amen.

Why Doesn't Grandpa Go to Church?
John 3:1-8

Adam was excited when he came home from spending the weekend with his grandparents. He wanted to tell his parents all the things that had happened. He told about the baseball game they went to on Saturday—and about the pizza they ate after the game.

"Grandma and I went to church," Adam said. "But Grandpa didn't go. Grandma says he never goes to church. Why doesn't Grandpa go to church?"

"I guess you'll have to ask Grandpa that," said Adam's father.

"I did ask him," said Adam. "But he talked about something else. Doesn't he love Jesus?"

"I don't know," said Adam's mother. "But I do know that Jesus loves Grandpa."

"Do you think Grandpa is mad at Jesus?" asked Adam. "If he is, would Jesus be mad at him?"

"No, Jesus always loves us," said his mother. "But some people don't know what Jesus has done for us. We tell you about Jesus so you know how he loves you. Then you can love him."

"Didn't anyone ever tell Grandpa about Jesus?" asked Adam.

"Some of us have tried," said his father, "but your grandfather doesn't want to listen to some things."

"Grandma says that Grandpa says he doesn't have to go to church to believe in God," said Adam.

"What do you think about that?" his father asked.

"I love God even when I'm not in church," said Adam, "but I still want to go."

"Let's look at it this way," said his mother. "Grandpa would be your grandfather even if you never went to see him. But since you love him, you want to go to his house and talk to him. There is only one God, whether we worship him or not. But since we love God, we want to go to church and worship him."

"Could I tell Grandpa that?" asked Adam.

"He might listen to you," said his father. "The important thing is for you to keep on loving your Grandpa and to keep on loving Jesus. Grandpa loves you. He might learn to love your friend Jesus too."

Some questions

Do you know people who do not show that they love Jesus?
Could it be that they love Jesus and you don't know it?
How could you find out if they love Jesus?
How could you help them love Jesus?

A prayer

Dear God, thank you for giving us faith in Jesus. Help us to share his love with others. Especially help _____ know that you love him (or her). Amen.

The Day Bobby Was Lost

Luke 2:41-52

The Ziller family will never forget June 17. They call it the day Bobby was lost.

Mr. Ziller had the day off from work, and he needed some paint for the back fence. Mrs. Ziller had seen an ad for a sale at her favorite shoe store. Since both parents needed to go to the shopping center, they took Emily, Suzanne, and Bobby along. When they parked the car, Emily said she wanted to go with her father. Suzanne said she wanted to go with her mother. Bobby said he wanted to go to the pet shop.

After a short discussion between the parents, which the children weren't allowed to hear, Bobby went to look at shoes with his mother and Suzanne. Actually, Mrs. Ziller and Suzanne looked at shoes; Bobby looked for gum under the seats in the shoe store.

The shoes on sale were not the kind Mrs. Ziller wanted, so she went to another store. Then another. At the third one she found a pair of feet-saver sandals. But she lost Bobby. She and Suzanne looked everywhere, but they couldn't find him.

"Maybe he went back to the car," suggested Suzanne. They rushed to the car and found Mr. Ziller, Emily, and two gallons of paint. But not Bobby.

"Hey, Mom lost Bobby," Suzanne yelled to the rest of the family and to the people getting into the car parked nearby.

"He wanted to go to the pet shop," said Emily. So they all ran to the pet store. Bobby was not there. Mrs. Ziller went back to the first two shoe stores. Mr. Ziller went to the toy store.

They did not find Bobby.

As Mrs. Ziller walked through a large department store on the way back to the car, she heard Bobby's name on the public address system. She stopped to listen as the announcement was repeated: "A five-year-old boy named Bobby is in the main office. His parents are lost. If they come to the office, Bobby will find them."

Mrs. Ziller found her husband and the girls. They ran to the office. There was Bobby eating a hot dog. Everyone hugged Bobby. Then they asked him questions: How did you get here? Why didn't you stay with us? Who bought the hot dog? Do you know what might happen to you if you ever do this again?

Mr. Ziller wanted to go home and paint the fence. But Emily and Suzanne didn't think it was fair for Bobby to have a hot dog when they were hungry. So the whole family went out for hot dogs to celebrate the day Bobby was found.

Bobby ate another hot dog, too.

Some questions

If you were lost in a crowd, whom would you ask for help?

Do you know your parents' full name(s), address, and phone number?

A prayer

Please help all children who get lost to be found again. Be with me so that I don't get lost. In Jesus' name. Amen.

Dad Lost His Job
Matthew 6:25-34

When Brad came home from school, he was surprised to find his father at home. He could see that his parents were worried.

"Hi, Brad!" said his father as he picked him up and held him on his lap.

"Hi, Dad!" he said and gave his father a hug. "Why are you home early?"

"I lost my job today, son," answered his father.

"What does that mean?" asked Brad.

"They laid off a lot of people where Daddy works," said his mother. "So he's out of a job."

"When will you go back to work?" asked Brad.

"I don't know, son," said his father. "It sounds like the company may close down."

"Does that mean we won't have anything to eat?" asked Brad.

"No," said his mother. "We will have food to eat. We will be very careful how we spend our money."

"I've got some money in my bank," said Brad. "You can use that."

"Thank you for wanting to help," said his father. "If we all work together we'll be all right. I will start looking for another job tomorrow."

"Maybe I can go back to work," said Brad's mother. "Then your daddy can stay home and take care of you and the baby."

"That would be fun, Dad," said Brad.

"And I'd like to be home with you," said his father.

"Are you and Mom worried?" asked Brad.

"Yes," said his father. "But we know God will help us. I have been out of work before, and I got another job. I'll get a new job soon."

"We want you to know what is happening, Brad," said his mother. "But we do not want you to worry. Our family is together, we can take care of each other, and God will look after us."

Some questions

Do you worry because you think one of your parents might lose a job?

Do you know someone whose mother or father has lost a job? How can you help other children whose parents do not have work?

A prayer

Dear God, thank you for those who have jobs in our family. Please help those who do not have jobs. Remind us that you love us, and teach us not to worry. In Jesus' name. Amen.

Will Mommy Die?
John 11:17-27

Lisa was afraid. Usually her mother would pick her up after school. But today her father would be there because her mother was in the hospital. She had been operated on at 10:00 that morning. Finally Lisa saw her father's car.

"Is Mommy OK?" she asked as she crawled into the front seat.

"The operation is over and everything went well," her father answered.

"Is she all right?" Lisa asked again.

"We're not sure," said her father as he reached over and held her hand. "She's fine for now. But she had a tumor. It might be cancer."

"Will Mommy die?" asked Lisa as tears ran down her face.

"No, I don't think so," said her father. "If she does have cancer, she will need to take treatments for a long time."

"What will happen to her?" asked Lisa.

"She may feel sick for a while," said her father. "But many people have had cancer and have gotten better again."

"But some have died," said Lisa.

"Yes, some have died," said her father. "But the doctor said he thinks your mother has a very good chance of being well and happy again."

"But what if she does die?" asked Lisa.

"We will all die sometime," said her father. "We've talked about dying before. Do you remember what happens when we die?"

"We go to live with Jesus," said Lisa.

"That's right," said her father. "Your mother and I have taught you about Jesus so that you can understand dying. When we are in church together, we hear how Jesus died to take away our sin. What happened after he died?"

"He came back to life," said Lisa.

"Right," said her father. "And he promises us that we will also live again, even after we die."

"I still don't want Mommy to die," said Lisa.

"I don't either," her father said. "And she doesn't either. She wants to stay with us. We'll ask God to make her well."

Some questions

Do you worry about anyone in your family being ill?

Do you know other children whose mother or father have died?

Can you talk to someone if you are worried about sickness or death?

A prayer

Father in heaven, be with all people who are ill and help them to get well. In Jesus' name. Amen.

What Makes You Angry?
James 1:19-20

"Are you happy?" asked Shane's mother as she tucked him in bed.

"Yes," he answered.

"Good, because there's something I want to talk to you about," said his mother. "Do you remember what happened when you came home from school today?"

"Nothing special," Shane answered.

"When you came in the door," said his mother, "you yelled at Fritz." Fritz was the family's dog.

"He jumped all over me and made me drop my books," said Shane. "He made me mad."

"That's what I want to talk to you about," said his mother. "I think you get angry about many things. You got angry at me because I wouldn't let you have a piece of pie."

"I was hungry," said Shane, "and I saw the pie in the refrigerator."

"I told you the pie was for dinner," said his mother, "and I offered you a banana. But you got angry and went off to your room and pouted. And do you remember what happened at dinner?"

"We ate the pie," said Shane.

"Yes, we did. But dinner was not fun for the family because you complained about your sister so many times."

"Well, she makes me mad," said Shane. "She smacks her lips when she eats, and she holds her fork funny."

"Don't you see that you get angry very easily?" said his mother. "Everyone gets angry sometimes, but anger can cause lots of problems. When you are angry, you say things that hurt others, and we can't talk to you. Do you remember when we took the trip with Uncle Art? Did you like to ride with him?"

"No," said Shane. "He yelled at all the other drivers and honked his horn at everyone."

"Uncle Art is always angry at people," said Shane's mother. "And he's not a happy person. You don't want to be like that, do you?"

"I didn't say the words he said," answered Shane.

"I know you didn't," said his mother. "And your daddy and I don't yell at you, because we don't like to get angry and make other people angry. We want to help you so that you won't become an angry person."

"But what if other people make me mad?" asked Shane.

"Other people don't make you angry," answered his mother. "You let yourself get angry over unimportant things. You don't have to get angry unless you want to."

"I'm not angry now," said Shane.

"And I'm not angry at you," said his mother.

Some questions

Why do people get angry?
Do you know people who get angry all the time?
Do you like to be with angry people?

A prayer

Lord Jesus, forgive me when I get angry at others and help me not to keep on being angry. Fill me with your love and forgiveness. Amen.

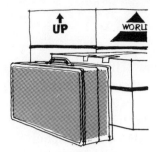

We're Moving to Albany!

Genesis 12:1-5

"After dinner we have something important to tell you," said Mr. Benson after the mealtime prayer as the family started to eat.

"Tell us now!" begged Paul. "Are we going to get a new car?"

"Are Grandpa and Grandma coming to see us?" asked Terri.

"No," said their father, "it's nothing like that. But maybe I had better tell you now. We're moving to Albany."

"Where's Albany?" asked Terri.

"It's a long way from here," answered Paul, who was in the sixth grade and knew lots of things. "Why do we have to move? I'd rather stay here."

"I've been offered a new job," said Mr. Benson. "It will help our family a lot if I take the job."

"It won't help me," said Paul. "I want to stay here."

"I want to move," said Terri. "Can we get a house with an upstairs and a swimming pool?"

"We don't know about those things yet," said their mother. "Your father and I are going to Albany next week. We'll look for a place to live."

"But I don't want to leave all my friends here," said Paul.

"We can make new friends in Albany," said Terri.

"You're just a little kid," Paul said to his sister. "You can play with anybody. But I have real friends!"

"We know that you like your school and friends here, Paul," said his mother. "We will help you make new friends in Albany."

"When will we move?" asked Terri.

"Maybe next month," said her father. "We have a lot of things to do before we move."

"Will we take our beds?" asked Terri.

"And the TV?" asked Paul.

"Of course," said their mother. "Those things will go in the moving van. But each of you can take one favorite thing with you in the car."

"I'll take my doll," said Terri.

"I'll take my friends, Brad and Jason," said Paul.

"Maybe Brad and Jason can come and visit you sometime," said his father. "Or maybe you can come back to visit them."

"OK," said Paul. "Then I'll take my baseball glove. Maybe I'll find someone in Albany who likes to play ball."

Some questions

(If your family has ever moved:) Are you glad you moved?

(If your family has never moved:) Do you think you will ever move to another home?

Do you have friends who have moved away? How can you help them?

Do you know anyone who has recently moved from another place to your community? Is there any way you can help them?

A prayer

Dear God, please help all people who are moving to a new home. Help them to make new friends. In Jesus' name. Amen.

I Don't Like My Name
Genesis 17:15-16

"Why did you give me my name?" asked Nicole as she rode with her mother on the way home from school. "It's such a dumb name!"

"I don't think Nicole is a dumb name," said her mother. "Your father and I thought it was a pretty name and we thought you were a pretty baby, so we named you Nicole."

"But everyone is named Nicole," she said. "Do you know there are two other Nicoles in my class at school?"

"That must be difficult for the teacher," said her mother, "but I guess other parents thought it was a pretty name too."

"And the kids tease me about my name," she said. "They call me Nickel, and they say, 'Nickel, Nickel, looks like a pickle.' "

"I guess kids always tease each other about their names," said her mother. "Do you know what other kids called me when I was little?"

"What did they call you?" asked Nicole.

"People now call me Pat, though my name is Patricia," said her mother. "But when I was little, everyone called me Patty. So the kids in my school called me Hamburger."

"Hamburger?" said Nicole.

"You know, 'Hamburger Patty,' " her mother said. "That used to make me so mad that I'd cry. So I wanted to give you a name that didn't sound like something to eat."

"If I have a little girl, I'll give her a very special name," said Nicole.

"Like what?"

"Astor Rowena sounds pretty to me," said Nicole. "Or maybe Contiabile Suzanne."

"Do you think she will like one of those names when she is your age?" asked her mother.

"I don't know," said Nicole. "But she can live with it, just like I have to live with mine."

"Well," said her mother, "I guess the most important thing is that God knows our names and that they are written in the book of life."

Some questions

Do you like your name? Do you think you will like your name when you grow up?

Does anyone ever tease you about your name? Do you tease others about their names?

A prayer

Dear God, help me to use my name so that it may mean good things to me and to others. In Jesus' name. Amen.

Run into Him, Dad!

Matthew 7:15-20

Matt and his father were driving home from a visit to the dentist. Suddenly a car pulled out of a driveway and drove right in front of their car.

"Run into him, Dad!" yelled Matt.

Matt's father slammed on the brakes and turned sharply to the right. He barely missed the other car. Both Matt and his father had their seatbelts on; so neither were hurt. The other car kept on going. Matt's father pulled to the side of the road and stopped the car.

"You missed him, Dad!" Matt said.

"Why did you want me to hit the other car?" his father asked.

"He drove in front of you," answered Matt. "It would have been his fault if you'd hit him."

"Maybe it would have been his fault," said his father, "but we would have been hurt, and our car would have been wrecked."

"You could have hit him," said Matt. "It wouldn't have hurt anything."

"Do you know how serious a car accident can be?" asked his father.

"I see lots of car accidents on TV," said Matt. "It's fun to see cars crash. No one gets hurt."

"That's what happens on TV," said his father. "But in real life, even a minor crash can hurt someone badly or even kill a person."

"Those wrecks on TV are real," said Matt. "They take pictures of real cars running into each other."

"No, son," said his father. "Those cars are made to look as if they are like other cars. But they are equipped to be wrecked. And the drivers are stuntmen who are trained to make a crash look real. The stuntmen wear special equipment to protect them when the cars crash."

"Are you sure?" asked Matt.

"Yes, Matt," answered his father. "Your mother and I do not like to have you watch that kind of program because you may not learn the difference between what is real and what is make-believe."

"I can tell the difference," said Matt. "When the dentist filled my tooth, that was a real pain."

"Right," said his father. "And that pain was small compared to the pain we would have right now if I had hit that car."

"OK," Matt said. "Let's go home—and don't hit anyone!"

Some questions

Can you always tell the things that are not real when you watch TV?

You know that all the problems of a TV show will be solved when the show is over. Does that happen in real life?

Do you think anyone should help you decide what programs to watch on TV? Who?

A prayer

Dear God, thank you for all the good things I can see on TV. Help me watch only those programs that will be good for me. In Jesus' name. Amen.

A Visit to the Dentist
Psalm 95:6-7

"What's that?" asked Cheri as she pointed at the chair on her first visit to a dentist.

"They call it a dentist's chair," said Dr. Elliott. "But I'm a dentist—and I never get to sit in it! So I think it is your chair. Do you want to sit in it?"

Cheri crawled into the chair. Dr. Elliott showed her how the chair moved up and down and how it could be tilted in different ways.

"Do you see this flashlight?" Dr. Elliott said as he pointed to a big light above the chair. "I bet your daddy doesn't have a flashlight that big."

Cheri watched as the dentist turned on the light and then picked up a tool with a long point on the end.

"Now I'm going to count your teeth," said Dr. Elliott. "How many teeth do you think you have?"

"I don't know," said Cheri.

"Guess."

"About ten," Cheri said.

"The only way we will find out is for me to count them," said Dr. Elliott. "Open your mouth wide. Let's see: one, two, three. . . ." As Dr. Elliott used a tool with a long point to touch each tooth, he also scraped around the tooth.

"I can see that you brush your teeth well," said the dentist. "Ten, eleven, twelve. . . but you left a little mess right there. I'll scrape it off for you."

Dr. Elliott continued to clean Cheri's teeth as he counted them, "Eighteen, nineteen, twenty. You have 20 teeth and one cavity. Do you know what a cavity is?"

"I don't know," said Cheri—though she remembered her mother had said she should brush her teeth well so she wouldn't have cavities.

"A cavity is a hole in your tooth," said the dentist. "But I will fill the hole for you. To do that, I will put your mouth to sleep. Please shut your eyes so I can put something in your mouth to make it go to sleep."

Cheri shut her eyes. Dr. Elliott rubbed her gums and then put something in her mouth. Soon her lip felt thick and numb.

"Now your tooth is asleep," said the dentist. "I'm going to use this machine to clean out the hole in your tooth. Here, you can hold it. It will make a noise, but it won't wake up your tooth. Open your mouth real wide so I can see all of your teeth."

Cheri shut her eyes as the doctor used the noisy machine to clean out the hole. Then he filled the hole with some grey paste. Her mouth felt strange but it did not hurt.

"I saw that hole, and now it is filled," said Dr. Elliott. "But you might have some other cavities that I can't see. So I'm going to take a picture of your teeth."

The dentist put a little piece of cardboard in her mouth. Then he told her, "When your daddy takes your picture, he asks you to stand very still. Now, if you hold your mouth very still, I'll snap the picture."

When Cheri left the dentist's office, her mouth felt funny. But she felt good. She knew Dr. Elliott liked her. She took the new toothbrush he had given her, and she promised him that she'd brush all 20 of her teeth twice a day.

Some questions

Have you ever thanked God for your teeth? And for your dentist?

Do you like to go to the dentist? Why or why not?

Your dentist helps you. How could you help him or her?

A prayer

Thank you, God, for creating me and for giving me many good things in my body. Help me take good care of all that you have given me. In Jesus' name. Amen.

He Called Me a Bad Name
Galatians 3:26-29

"How do you like your new school?" Mr. Warner asked his son after their first day in a new neighborhood.

"One of the kids called me a bad name," answered Chad.

"What did he call you?" asked his father.

"The teacher said it is a dirty word and I shouldn't even say it," said Chad. "She said he called me that because I'm black."

55

"Are there other black children in your school?" asked Mr. Warner.

"There are some in school, but not in my room," answered Chad. "Why do they have a bad name for black people?"

"A name doesn't make people bad," his father said. "But it's bad to call people names. The boy who called you that name didn't hurt you; he hurt himself."

"Is there a bad word that I can call him?" asked Chad.

"There are bad names for others," Mr. Warner said, "but I don't want you to learn them. People have bad names for every race and nationality. They use words like that when they want to pretend they are better than others."

"If that white kid called me a bad name, can't I call him one too?" asked Chad.

"No," said his father. "If you did, you would have done something just as bad as what he did. If you don't call him a bad name, he may learn to stop calling others bad names."

"Will people ever stop using those bad words?" asked Chad.

"I doubt it," said his father. "But sometimes things get better. When your grandfather was a boy, he heard the bad word for black people all the time. When I was young, I often heard it. But you haven't heard it until today. So things are getting better."

"Yeah," said Chad. "Maybe my kids won't hear it at all."

Some questions

How many different races or nationalities of people go to your school? to your church? are living in your neighborhood?

If all the people in your community are of the same race, do you know about other races from watching television?

Does God love all people the same?

A prayer

Dear Jesus, thank you for loving all of us. Help us to love all other people. Amen.

Why Did He Have Those Pictures?

Genesis 3:1-7

Dale's father was painting the bedroom walls. Dale was helping him. He liked to work with his dad.

"Dad, when I was over at Scott's house on Saturday," said Dale, "he showed me a magazine that his dad had hidden in the garage."

"What kind òf magazine was it?" his father asked.

"It had a lot of pictures of women with no clothes on," said Dale, "and some men too. Why did he have those pictures?"

Dale's father put the brush down and sat on the ladder. "Do you think his dad wanted Scott to see those pictures?" he asked.

"He hid them," said Dale. "But Scott found them."

"Why do you think he hid them?" his father asked.

"Because he was ashamed of them," answered Dale.

"Right!" said his father. "Were you ashamed of looking at them?"

"Yes," said Dale. "But I didn't look very much."

"I'm glad you didn't," said his father. "Even people who don't like such pictures will look. I'm glad you told me about the pictures. You're old enough to understand why your mother and I don't have things like that in our house."

"I'm glad you don't," said Dale.

"We want you to know that our bodies are beautiful," said his father. "God created us. And he made us beautiful. So you never need to be ashamed of your body."

"Then why were those pictures bad?" asked Dale.

"They were bad because they made the body seem dirty," said his father. "Not dirty like we get when we work, but dirty in the mind. Instead of seeing the beauty of the body, it made you feel embarrassed and ashamed."

"I wouldn't want anyone to take pictures of me without my clothes on," said Dale.

"That's right," his father said.

"Didn't we see pictures and statues of people without clothes on at the art museum when we were on vacation?" said Dale.

"Yes," said his father. "But were they like the pictures in the magazine you saw?"

"No," said Dale.

"They were different," said his father, "because they showed that the body is beautiful. The ones in the magazine showed the body in a dirty way. People feel like hiding those pictures. Hey, my paintbrush is getting dry. I've got to get to work."

"OK," said Dale. "I'll help you."

Some questions

What should you do if your friends show you pictures that they would not want their parents or teachers to see?

Do you know when it is right for someone (like a doctor) to see or touch your body, and when it is not right?

What can you do to help yourself feel good about your body?

A prayer

Almighty God, thank you for creating me and others, and for saving us through Jesus. Help us all to take good care of our bodies. Amen.

She Looks Just Like My Great-Grandmother
Leviticus 19:32

Kara, Robyn, and Stacy were walking home from school. An old woman came down the same street.

"Look at that funny old lady," said Robyn. "She walks like a little baby."

"She's ugly," said Kara. "Her skin looks like an elephant's. Look at all those wrinkles!"

"What a funny dress she's wearing!" said Robyn. "Look how it hangs all over."

"You shouldn't say those things," said Stacy. "She'll hear you."

"So what if she hears us!" said Kara. "She's a crazy old lady. Besides, I bet she can't hear a thing."

"She probably can't see, either," said Robyn.

"I think she's nice," said Stacy.

"Nice?" asked Robyn. "What's nice about her?"

"She reminds me of my great-grandma," said Stacy.

"Who is your great-grandma?" asked Robyn.

"That's my daddy's grandmother," said Stacy. "She lives in a nursing home, and we go to see her every week."

"And she looks like that old lady?" asked Kara.

"Yes," said Stacy. "She's very old. She can't walk unless someone helps her. Her skin is wrinkled, and she can't hear very well. But I think she's pretty."

"That doesn't sound pretty to me," said Robyn.

"She's pretty when you get to know her," said Stacy. "She likes to see me, and she likes anything I make for her. She tells me stories about when she was a little girl, and she likes to hear about what I do."

"She sounds nice," said Kara.

"She *is* nice!" said Stacy. "Do you think that old lady is someone's great-grandmother?"

"Maybe," said Kara. "But maybe not. If she's not, she might like to talk to someone else's little kids."

"Let's go and ask if we can carry her grocery sack for her," said Stacy.

Some questions

Who is the oldest person you know?
How can you make older people happier?
How can older people make you happier?

A prayer

Dear God, bless all older people, and help them to be happy. I especially ask you to help _____ . In Jesus' name. Amen.

Should We Keep It?

Exodus 20:1-2, 15

"Hey! Look!" yelled Alicia to her friend Julie as they walked home from school. Julie looked at the place where Alicia was pointing. At first she didn't see anything but leaves. Then she noticed a wallet lying on the ground.

"Someone must have lost it," said Alicia as she ran over to pick it up. The two girls quickly opened it.

"Look at all that money," said Alicia.

"There's a lot. Let's count it," said Julie. "There's two ten-dollar bills. That's $20.00. And a five and three ones. That's $28.00."

"Wow! That's a lot of money—and we get to keep it," said Alicia.

"Not if we can find out who it belongs to," said Julie.

"Yes, we can keep it," said Alicia. "I've heard people say: 'Finders keepers, losers weepers.' "

"No, first we have to see if we can find who it belongs to," said Julie. "I bet it has a name in it somewhere."

"You don't have to look for a name," said Alicia.

"Here!" said Julie. "It belongs to Ronald Smith. He lives at 9600 Flagler. And here's his phone number."

"I bet if you give it back to him, he won't even say thank-you for finding it," said Alicia.

"I think he will," Julie said. "Besides, that doesn't make any difference. It belongs to him, and we should give it back."

"But I saw it first," said Alicia, "It's really mine."

"But you showed it to me, so we both found it," said Julie. "And I say we call this phone number and tell the man we found his wallet."

"I'll divide the money with you," said Alicia.

"But the money isn't ours," said Julie. "If you had been by yourself and found it, would you have kept it for yourself?"

"I don't know," said Alicia. "I might have."

"That would have been stealing. And that's wrong," said Julie.

"Oh, OK," said Alicia. "Let's phone him. I hope he gives us a reward."

Some questions

If you had found the wallet, would you have phoned the owner?

If you lost something, would you want the person who found it to return it to you?

Do you have your phone number on your wallet, purse, toys, or other things you might lose?

A prayer

Lord Jesus, help me be honest when I take care of other people's things, and help them be honest when they take care of mine. Amen.

You Can't Hug a Daydream
Philemon 8-16

Tim's dad had been away on a business trip for four days. During the day Tim was busy with school and friends, so he didn't think about his father being gone. But at night he missed talking to his dad and sitting on his knee. He couldn't wait until he came home again.

Tim had heard his mother say that his dad would be home on Friday. But when Tim came home from school, he wasn't there. He asked his mother when his dad would be home.

"He'll get here about 10:00 tonight," his mother said.

"Can I stay up until he gets home?" Tim asked.

"No, you can't stay up that late, even on Friday night," his mother said. "You'll see him tomorrow."

Tim begged her to let him stay up late. Finally, his mother said that if he went to bed at 8:00 she would ask his father to come in and talk to him a little bit when he got home.

Tim went to sleep thinking about his dad. Later he felt his dad's hand on his head.

"Hi, son!" his dad said, "I'm home."

"I'm *so* glad to see you," said Tim as he sat up and hugged his father.

"I'm glad to see you too, Tim," said his dad.

"Dad, I missed you so much when you were gone," said Tim.

"I missed you too, son," said his father. "But you know I love you even when I'm gone."

"I know that, Dad," said Tim. "But you can't hug a daydream."

Tim's dad was quiet for a long time as he held the boy on his lap. Finally he said, "You're right, Tim. We can't hug daydreams. What you said may help me. I will always have to travel a lot on my job. Will it help if I give you extra hugs on the days I am home?"

"I think so," said Tim.

"Maybe there's something else we can do," his father said. "Do you say a prayer when you eat lunch at school?"

"Yes," Tim answered.

"I also say a prayer before I eat lunch when I'm on a business trip. Would it help if I included you in my prayer, and you included me in your prayer?"

"It might," said Tim.

"When each of us prays, we will know that Jesus is with both of us. He's with you at school and he's with me at work."

"I can hug Jesus so he can hug you for me," said Tim. "And you can hug Jesus so he can hug me for you."

"Now it's time for you to go back to sleep," his father said.

"But first, a hug!" said Tim.

Some questions

Does your mother's or father's job keep them from being with you as much as they would like?

How can you let them know you love them even when they are not with you?

A prayer

Thank you, God, for the times that our family can be together. Help us love each other. In Jesus' name. Amen.

Bad Words

James 3:10-11

Jimmy looked sad and worried when he came home from school. He handed a note from his teacher to his mother. "Do you know what this note says?" asked his mother.

"I think so," Jimmy answered. "It says I used bad words in school today."

"Yes, that's what the teacher says," said his mother. "Do you know which bad words you said?"

"Yes," said Jimmy.

"Do you know why the words are bad?" his mother asked him.

"I guess because the teacher didn't like them," answered Jimmy.

"No," said his mother. "What the teacher likes or doesn't like is not what makes some words bad. The words are bad because they do bad things to people and to God. Did you know that words can do things?"

"No," said Jimmy.

"Words can do many things," his mother said. "Some words make us happy. Some words make us scared. Some words make us laugh. Others make us cry. Most words are good because they help us learn things or they tell others how we feel. But some words are bad because they hurt people."

64

Jimmy didn't say anything. He thought about the words he had said.

"Do you think the words you said hurt anyone?" his mother asked.

"Yes," Jimmy said. "I called Amy a bad name. She cried."

"The words you said hurt Amy," said his mother. "Do you think they hurt anyone else?"

"My teacher didn't like what I said," Jimmy answered. "Did the words hurt her?"

"Yes," his mother said. "And me too. The words you said hurt me. But the words you said hurt someone else even more than Amy, your teacher, or me. Do you know who else they hurt?"

"No," said Jimmy.

"The bad words you said hurt *you*, Jimmy," his mother said. "The bad words you used to hurt Amy really hurt you more than they hurt her. Others who heard you probably felt sorry for Amy. What you said told more about you than it did about her."

"I'm sorry, Mom," said Jimmy.

"And I forgive you, Jimmy," said his mother. "The Bible tells us that good words and bad words come out of the same mouth. Jesus forgives us when we say bad words. He paid for our bad words when he died on the cross for us."

"I'm glad!" Jimmy said.

"So am I!" said his mother. "But Jesus does even more. He helps us say good words. But now it's time for us to get dinner ready. Tomorrow we'll talk about good words, OK?"

Later

Some questions

Have other people said words to you that have hurt you?

Have you hurt other people with words?

How can you take away the hurt other people feel from your words?

A prayer

Jesus, forgive me when I have used words to hurt others. Help me forgive others who have hurt me. Amen.

Good Words
Proverbs 15:1-2

Jimmy was happy when he came home from school. His mother was waiting for him.

"Do you have a note from the teacher for me today, Jimmy?" his mother asked.

"No," he answered. But he remembered the note he had brought home the day before. The teacher had told his mother he had used bad words in school.

"I wasn't expecting another note about bad words today," his mother said. "But we said we'd talk about something else today, remember?"

"Today we talk about good words."

"Right!" his mother said. "If some words are bad because they hurt people, why are some words good?"

"Because they help people," Jimmy answered.

"Yes," said his mother. "Good words make people happy. What words make you feel good?"

"Dinner's ready," said Jimmy.

"Those are happy words for me, too," said his mother. "Those words tell us God has given us food to eat. I'm also happy that we can eat together as a family."

"I know another good word," said Jimmy.

"What is it?" his mother asked.

"We," Jimmy answered.

"Why is *we* a good word?" his mother asked.

"Because it means I'm not alone. When I say 'we,' I mean someone is with me."

"You're right, Jimmy," said his mother. *"We* is a happy word. *Love* is also a good word."

"And *help* is a good word. So is *sunshine.*"

"But *rain* is also a good word," said his mother. "Most words are good words when we use them the right way. I think *Jesus* is the best word of all. Do you know why?"

"Because he loves us and helps us," said Jimmy.

"Right!" his mother said. "When we know Jesus is with us;

we use words that are good. That makes other people happy—
and it makes us happy too. It's more fun to be with people who
use good words."

"Did you use good words at school today, Jimmy?"

"Yes," said Jimmy. "School was more fun today than yesterday."

Some questions

Do you know people who always use kind words? Who?

What words do you use that make other people happy?

Would you rather be with people who use good words or
those who use bad words?

A prayer

Dear God, thank you for giving love to others so that they
can say good words to me. Help me say good words to others.
Amen.

Who Got Nicole into Trouble?
Romans 15:1-5

Nicole had invited her two best friends, Jenny and Crystal,
to her house after school. Jenny's mother was going to pick
them up after dinner, so they would have a long time to play.

But Nicole had to stay after school. Jenny and Crystal did
not want to go home, so they sat and waited for Nicole.

Finally, Nicole came out to look for them. They walked to
Nicole's house together.

"Boy, am I mad at Sandy," said Nicole.

"What did she do?" asked Jenny.

"It's her fault I had to stay after school. Now my mother will
yell at me, and we won't have as much time to play. It's all
Sandy's fault."

"What did she do?" asked Crystal.

"She told on me," said Nicole. "She's a tattletale."

"What did she say?" asked Crystal.

"She told the teacher that I threw water on the little kids in the bathroom."

"Did you?" asked Jenny.

"Yes. They were making too much noise."

"Why did Sandy tell on you?" asked Jenny.

"Because the teacher asked her who did it," answered Nicole.

"Did the teacher ask you who did it?" asked Jenny.

"She asked everybody. No one told on me except Sandy."

"Then Sandy was the only one who told the truth," said Jenny. "It's not her fault you had to stay after school. It's your fault because you threw water on the little kids."

"But the teacher wouldn't have known if Sandy hadn't told on me."

"Did you want Sandy to tell a lie?" asked Jenny.

"She didn't have to get me in trouble," said Nicole.

"Sandy didn't get you into trouble," said Crystal. "You got yourself into trouble because you threw the water."

"You're not my friends if you aren't on my side," said Nicole.

"We *are* your friends," said Crystal. "But we don't think you should lie. If you do something wrong, you should admit it and not blame other people."

"You sound like my mother!" said Nicole.

"In Sunday school they told us that if you do something wrong, you admit it," said Crystal. "Jesus forgives us when we admit we did something wrong."

"Are you mad at me because I had to stay after school?" asked Nicole.

"No, we're not mad at you," said Crystal. "You're our friend. But if you know Jesus forgives you, you don't have to blame Sandy. And you don't have to be mad anymore. And then we can have fun again."

"I like that," said Nicole. "Let's run home!"

Some questions

Do you agree that Nicole got herself into trouble?

If you do something wrong and someone tells on you, who causes you to get into trouble?

68

Does it help if you blame someone else when you do something wrong?

A prayer

Lord Jesus, help me to see my own faults and the things I do that are wrong. Thank you for dying for me and for forgiving my sins. Amen.

Are You Going to Leave Us?
Romans 8:31-35

Adam's father was tucking him in bed.

"Are you worried about something, son?" he asked.

"Yes," said Adam as tears came to his eyes.

"What's the matter, Adam?" said his father.

"Are you going to leave us?" Adam asked.

"What do you mean?" said his father.

"I mean, are you going to move to another house?" Adam asked with tears rolling down his cheek.

"Of course not, son. Why do you ask?" his father said.

"Brian's dad doesn't live with them anymore," said Adam. "He lives in an apartment. Brian and his sister go to visit him on weekends."

"I'm sorry to hear that," said his father.

"And I heard you say Uncle Roger and Aunt Ellen got a divorce. That means they don't live together anymore, doesn't it?" asked Adam.

"Yes, that's what it means," his father said.

"Does that mean you might not live with us anymore either?"

"No, son," his father said as he hugged him. "I want to live with you and your mother for a long time."

"Why did Uncle Roger and Brian's father move away?"

"Uncle Roger still loves your cousins," said his father. "And you said that Brian sees his father often."

"But why did they have to get a divorce?" asked Adam.

"Divorce is a hard thing to understand, Adam," his father

said. "But Uncle Roger did not divorce your cousins. He is still their father, and Aunt Ellen is still their mother."

"I know," said Adam. "But it would be better for them to live together."

"Yes, it would," said his father. "That's why God has told us not to get a divorce. Divorce hurts people. God does not want us to be hurt."

"Then why do people get divorces?" asked Adam.

"Sometimes people don't do what is best," his father answered. "We all do wrong things; and when we do, we hurt ourselves and others—just like divorces have hurt Brian and your cousins. But Jesus can forgive and help people even after they do things that are wrong."

"Does Jesus still love Brian's mother and father and Uncle Roger and Aunt Ellen?" asked Adam.

"Of course he does!" said his father. "And he loves Brian and your cousins too. Jesus helps mothers and fathers to take care of their children, even after a divorce. And you can help Brian and your cousins too."

"How?"

"By helping them to love both their parents," his father said. "You can also help them not to worry by showing that you care about them."

"I'll try," said Brian.

"Are you ready to pray?" his father asked.

"Yes."

Some questions

Have you ever been afraid that your parents would get a divorce?

If your parents are divorced, do you want to talk about it with them?

A prayer

Dear God, bless our family, and help us to love and forgive one another. Keep us together. Be with all families that have had a divorce. Help the children, the fathers, and the mothers, so that they may all stay close to you. In Jesus' name. Amen.

A Day to Remember

Psalm 9:1-2

Laura was too excited to sleep. Her mother had told her twice to turn out the light and settle down, but Laura found one more reason to hop out of bed.

"You've had such a big day," said her mother as she walked the girl back to her bed again. "You should be glad to go to sleep."

"I'm too excited to sleep," said Laura.

"Then let's talk about why you are excited," her mother said.

"I had fun today, and I like to think about it," said Laura.

"Well, I had fun today, too," her mother said, "and I like to think about it. What was the most fun for you?"

"Most of all I liked being on all the rides," said Laura, "especially the boats going down the waterfalls, and the horses, and the ride that went up and down and round and round. What did you like best, Mom?"

"I liked being with my family," said her mother, "and I liked seeing all of you laughing, and I liked the monkey show."

"I liked those things too," said Laura, "and the hamburgers and the ice cream."

"This was a day to remember," her mother said.

"Yes," said Laura. "See, I have this picture and this flag. I'm going to put them on my wall so I can always remember today."

"I'm glad you had such a nice day," said her mother. "We planned this day so you would have a good memory of being with the family. I remember happy days from when I was a little girl. I want you to have happy memories too."

"I don't want to forget today," said Laura.

"If you think about it often, then you will always remember it," her mother said. "And I know another way to help you remember today."

"How?" Laura asked.

"By thanking God for such a fun day. Jesus was with us today," said her mother.

"Why was he with us today?" asked Laura. "Everything was going fine."

"We need him on good days too," her mother said. "Our family was happy today because we could be together and show our love for one another. Jesus gives us that love. He forgives the things that could make us angry and ruin a nice day. And he helps us to be thankful for the many things we enjoy."

"Can we thank Jesus now?" asked Laura.

"We sure can!" said her mother.

Some questions

Do you remember a special day when you were very happy?

Are you looking forward to any special day?

What can you do to help other people have a happy day?

A prayer

Dear Jesus, thank you for a fun day. Thank you for my family and the things we do together. Help us always to love one another. Bless other families too. Amen.

Where's My Present?

Acts 2:38-39

Mark sat at the window watching for the mail to be delivered. It was his birthday, and he knew he would get a present from his grandparents. He liked to receive gifts. It was fun to look at the packages with their special wrappings, to shake them, and to guess what was in them.

When the mail came, there wasn't a package. But there was an envelope addressed to Mark. It was from his grandparents. Mark was disappointed.

"Where's my present?" Mark asked his mother.

"This is your present," Mark's mother explained. "The letter says that Grandpa and Grandma have put $500 in your education fund. It will collect interest and help pay for your college education later."

"But I wanted a present now," said Mark.

"It *is* a present for you now," said his mother. "It shows you that your grandparents love you. It shows they are thinking about your future."

"But I can't see it," said Mark.

"Some of the most important gifts you have are those you can't see," said his mother.

"Like what?" asked Mark.

"Like when you believe in Jesus," his mother said.

"What do I get then?" asked Mark.

"When you believe in Jesus, your sins are forgiven and you receive the gift of the Holy Spirit," said his mother.

"What does that mean?" asked Mark.

"The Holy Spirit gives you a new life," his mother said. "In that new life your sins are forgiven because of what Jesus did for you."

"I can't see that," said Mark.

"That's true," said his mother. "But it's real. Just as your grandparent's gift will earn interest for you every day, the gift that God gives you through Jesus is a part of your life every day. You belong to God."

"Then Grandma and Grandpa didn't forget me?" asked Mark.

"Of course not," said his mother. "They remembered you in a very special way."

Some questions

Name some gifts that are only for today. Name some that are only for the future. Name some that are for both now and the future.

God forgives your sins because of Jesus. What does that tell you about your future?

God gave Jesus to be your Savior. Is that a gift for now, for the future, or for both?

I'm Afraid of Thunder and Lightning

Revelation 4:5; 8:5

A bolt of lightning flashed across the sky, and the loud rumble of thunder followed. Kevin ran into the house crying for his mother. His mother knew that Kevin was afraid of thunder and lightning. She held him on her lap as he cried.

"You'll be all right," said his mother. "I am with you. God is with us both."

"I'm scared," sobbed Kevin. "The lightning will kill us or kill Daddy."

"No, the lightning will not kill us," his mother said.

"But it has killed some people," said Kevin. "God could use it to kill us too."

"Yes, lightning has killed some people," said his mother. "But God does not use lightning to kill people. He wants us to live. The lightning killed people, but God didn't kill them."

"But God makes the thunder and lightning," said Kevin.

"Yes, but God did not make it to kill people," his mother said. "When lightning does kill someone, we know God still loves that person. Remember, Jesus died for us. He took away our punishment. God does not use lightning to kill people."

"Then why does God make thunder and lightning?" asked Kevin.

"You asked me that during the last storm," said his mother, "so I looked for some answers. First, lightning puts something into the soil that helps crops grow. We need rain and sunshine to grow the food we eat. We also need lightning."

"You mean lightning is good?" asked Kevin.

"Yes," his mother said. "Look at the lightning flash now! And there's the thunder that is made by the lightning! God is helping the farmers with their crops. Lightning and thunder are pretty to see and hear if you know God is helping us."

"I don't think so," said Kevin.

"I also checked what the Bible said about lightning," his mother said. "Do you know there will be lightning in heaven? If you want to read about it, look at Revelation 4:5 and 8:5."

"And nothing will hurt us in heaven," said Kevin.

"That's right," said his mother. "And lightning also has another good purpose."

"What?" asked Kevin.

"It reminds us that Jesus is coming," his mother said. "Jesus said, 'For as the lightning comes from the east and flashes to the west, so will be the coming of the Son of Man' " (Matthew 24:27).

"But lots of people are scared of thunder and lightning," said Kevin.

"Yes, they are," said his mother. "But you don't have to be afraid. We have taught you what to do when a storm comes. Stay away from tall metal things. Don't stand under trees."

"I can do that," said Kevin.

"And whenever you are scared of something, it's always good to pray," his mother said. "Would you like me to pray with you now?"

"Yes!" Kevin said.

Some questions

Are you afraid of lightning and thunder? Do you know someone who is?

What should you do to protect yourself from lightning?

What can you enjoy about lightning?

A Happy Way to Cry
Genesis 46:28-30

"Why are you sad on your birthday?" Chris asked his mother.

"I'm not sad," said his mother. "In fact, I'm very happy."

"I saw you cry at the table," said Chris. Everyone in the family had given her a birthday gift, and they all had sung "Happy Birthday" to her after dinner. "And I saw tears in Daddy's eyes too," Chris said.

"Yes, you saw us both cry tonight," his mother said. "But do you know why we cried?"

"Because you are sad," said Chris.

"Sometimes we cry because we are sad," said his mother. "But there are other reasons for crying. Do you cry at other times?"

"Yes," said Chris. "I cry when I'm hurt."

"So do I," said his mother. "I also cry when I'm angry."

"And when I'm scared," added Chris.

"Now you know all the reasons why I *didn't* cry," his mother said. "I'm not sad or angry or scared. I don't hurt."

"Then why did you cry?" asked Chris.

"Because I'm very happy," his mother said.

"You cry because you're happy?" asked Chris.

"Yes," she said, "Your daddy and I are so happy to have you and the rest of our family. You made us happy when you showed how you loved us."

"We didn't want to make you cry," said Chris.

"You made us very happy," she said as.she hugged Chris. "You made me remember the time when I was a little girl and gave birthday presents to my mother."

"Will I cry when I remember giving birthday presents to you?" asked Chris.

"You may," said Mother. "If you do, they will be happy tears because today was a very happy day."

"Do you cry every time you are happy?" asked Chris.

"No," his mother said. "Sometimes I laugh. Sometimes I sing. Sometimes I just feel good."

"I saw you cry in church once," Chris said.

"Those were happy tears too," said his mother. "I thought about how much Jesus loves us. I remembered how he is with us and takes care of us. I was so happy that I cried."

"Should I cry when I'm happy?" asked Chris.

"You can, but you don't have to," said his mother. "Each person is different. I want you to be happy. That's why I tell you I love you. That's why I tell you Jesus loves you. I'm happy when I see you happy."

"I'm happy now," said Chris.

"Good," said his mother. "So you've given me a happy birthday. Thanks!"

Some questions

What do you do when you are happy?

Can you tell when others in your family are happy?

How can you make other people happy?

A prayer

Dear God, give us a happy family and help us enjoy each other. In Jesus' name. Amen.

It's No Big Deal to Lose

Romans 5:3-5

"Come on, Jimmy!" yelled Brad as he picked up his ball and glove. "It's time to go."

"I don't want to go," replied Jimmy.

"What do you mean, you don't want to go? You've got to go because I'm taking care of you and I'm playing ball."

"I don't like to play ball," said Jimmy.

"What's the matter with you?" his older brother said. "Last week you pestered and pestered me because you wanted to play ball with me and my friends. Now I ask you to play, and you don't want to."

"I just don't want to," answered Jimmy.

"If you don't play, I don't get to play," said Brad. "Mom said I had to take care of you today. Come on, let's go!"

Jimmy was quiet for a while. Then a tear rolled down his cheek.

"Hey, what's wrong?" asked his big brother.

"I'm no good. I can't play ball," said Jimmy.

"Last week you told me you were going to play for the Giants when you grew up," said Brad.

"But I struck out twice," said Jimmy. "And I dropped the only catch that came to left field."

"Is that so bad?" asked Brad.

"Your friends laughed at me. They called me a klutz."

"So what?" said Brad. "They're all four years older than you are. Do you think they'd look so good if they played on a high school team?"

"I guess not," said his little brother.

"You'd be the best player on the team if you played with the little kids in daycare," said Brad.

"Maybe I *should* play with them," said Jimmy. "Then I could win all the time."

"Sure, you might win," said Brad, "but you wouldn't learn to play ball any better. It's no big deal to lose if you play against a better team. That's how you get better at playing ball."

Jimmy went along to play ball with Brad and his friends. He still made some outs, but once in a while he hit the ball. He still dropped the ball sometimes, but he also caught it once in a while.

Jimmy learned how to play ball—and he also learned something else. He learned that he didn't have to be the best at everything. God had given him the ability to do some things. But God also gave other people the ability to do other things. Jimmy learned to do what he could—when he could. When he couldn't do something, he learned to depend on someone else.

Some questions

Can you learn something when you make a mistake?
Do you think you should be able to do everything right?
How can you help someone who makes a mistake?

A prayer

Jesus, help me know what I can do, and help me learn to do those things better. Help me know what I cannot do. Amen.

Look What You Found!
Luke 15:8-10

Seth's father was happy as he waited for his son to come back from a school trip. He knew that Seth had looked forward to the trip. He was surprised when he saw tears running down Seth's face when the boy got off the bus.

"What's wrong, Seth?" his father asked.

"I didn't have any fun at all," sobbed Seth as they got in the car.

"What went wrong?" asked his father.

"I lost my wallet—the one Grandma gave me," said Seth. "And I lost the 10 dollars you gave me for the trip. I didn't have any fun at all because I couldn't buy anything."

"Did you have anything to eat?" his father asked.

"Some of the kids and the teacher shared their lunch with me," said Seth. "But I didn't get to buy anything, and I didn't get to go on all the rides. I lost everything."

"You lost your wallet and money," said his father, "but you also found something that might be more important."

"I didn't find anything," sobbed Seth.

"You found out that your friends would help you. They bought you something to eat," his father said.

"Everyone was nice to me," said Seth. "The teacher bought one ticket for me, so I had one ride. Jason bought me an ice cream cone."

"So you *did* find something," said his father. "You found that friends will help you. And I think you found something else."

"What?" asked Seth.

"You found that things aren't as important as people," his father said. "I'm sorry you lost the money. But you're more important than the money. I'm glad you weren't hurt."

"So am I," said Seth.

"You may also be finding out how to live with disappointment," said his father. "All of us have bad things happen to us. We have to learn how not to let one bad thing ruin many good things."

"I liked the bus ride," said Seth. "And I liked being out of school all day. And I liked seeing lots of things."

"You lost your money and a wallet," said his father, "but look at all the things you found. Maybe it was worth it. Did you remember to ask God to help you?"

"I asked him to help me find the money," said Jason, "but he didn't find it for me."

"That's because God helped you in another way," said his father. "He helped you find things more important than money. And he gave you Jesus, who is the most important part of your life. By the way, I found something today too."

"What did you find, Dad?" asked Seth.

"I found that having a son who can talk to me is worth much more than 10 dollars," said his father.

Some questions

Have you been sad because you lost something?

Do you know others who are sad because they lost something?

What did you learn when you lost something that was important to you?

A prayer

Dear God, help me take good care of the things you have given me. In Jesus' name. Amen.

No One Likes Me
Psalm 28:1-3

Mrs. Watkins took her class out to the playground for recess. She watched the students as they played and noticed that Jennifer was standing all alone.

"Hi, Jennifer," her teacher said. "Would you like to play with some of the others?"

"No," said Jennifer.

"Recess is a good time to play," said Mrs. Watkins. "I bet you'd like to kick the ball with those kids over there."

"They don't want me to play with them," said Jennifer.

"Why not?" Mrs. Watkins asked.

"Because they don't like me!" Jennifer answered.

"Why do you think they don't like you?" asked Mrs. Watkins.

"Because I'm too shy," said Jennifer.

"Yes, you are shy," said her teacher. "Do you think that is bad?"

"Of course it's bad," Jennifer said. "No one likes me."

"I like you," said Mrs. Watkins.

"You have to like me because you're my teacher," said Jennifer.

"No, I like you because you are you," said Mrs. Watkins. "Being shy is a part of who you are—just like being tall is a part of who I am. Do you know that I am taller than most women?"

"Yes," said Jennifer, "but you are pretty and nice."

"Thank you," said Mrs. Watkins. "Some women might not like to be as tall as I am. But I like it because that's who I am. Maybe you are more shy than many people. But that's who you are, and I like you."

"But I can't have many friends," said Jennifer.

"Of course you can have friends," said Mrs. Watkins.

"Look at the children over there. See how good Susie is at playing ball. She's a good leader. What if everyone in the class were a leader like Susie?"

"I wish I were like her," said Jennifer.

"But if you were like her, I would miss knowing you," said Mrs. Watkins. "I'm glad that the class has many different kinds of boys and girls. Some can sing. Some are good readers. Some are good at playing sports. You are good at math. Each of you has something very special about you."

"But no one likes me," said Jennifer.

"They don't dislike you," said Mrs. Watkins. "They just don't know you because you are shy. But you can fix that. Let them find out that you are a kind and gentle person. You don't have to *make* them like you; you can *let* them like you."

"How?" asked Jennifer.

"By liking them," Mrs. Watkins said. "If you like other people for who *they* are, they can like you for who *you* are."

"I don't have to be like Susie to have friends?" asked Jennifer.

"No, let Susie be Susie," said her teacher. "You be Jennifer. We need you to be who you are."

Some questions

If you could change anything about yourself, what would you change?

Can you be happy with yourself as you are?

You can change how you act and how you take care of your appearance. Is that more important than the things you can't change?

A prayer

Thank you, heavenly Father, for creating me. Help me accept myself as the person you made me, and help me to become the person you want me to be. In Jesus' name. Amen.

There's Nothing Wrong with Dying
1 Corinthians 15:20-22

Jeremy sat at the window for a long time and watched the house next door. He knew that Mrs. Morris had died. He saw many people going in and out of the house. Some carried bowls of food or flowers. Some were crying.

"Are you thinking about Mrs. Morris?" asked Jeremy's father as he sat down beside him.

"Yes," said Jeremy. "Why did she die, Daddy?"

"Because she had cancer," his father said.

"But she wasn't old," said Jeremy.

"No, Jeremy, Mrs. Morris was younger than I am."

"I thought only old people died," said Jeremy, "like when Grandpa died last year."

"Young people can die too," his father said, "even babies."

"I don't want you to die," said Jeremy.

"And I don't want you to die, either," said his father. "If I do die, I want you to know there's nothing wrong with dying."

"My Sunday school teacher said the wages of sin is death [Romans 6:23]. Did Mrs. Morris die because she did something bad?"

"No," his father said. "Jesus paid the wages of sin when he died for us. The rest of that Bible verse says, '. . .the gift of God is eternal life in Christ Jesus our Lord.' God gave Mrs. Morris a gift when she died. He took her to heaven with him."

83

"Will we go to heaven when we die?" asked Jeremy.

"Yes, son, we will," said his father. "I think I will live a long time. But when I do die, I want you to remember that I believe in Jesus as my Lord and Savior. Then you will know I am in heaven with him."

"I believe in Jesus too," said Jeremy.

"I'm glad you can tell me that," his father said. "I think you will live a long, long time. But I'm glad you know about Jesus now. He also helps us live here. Would you like to go to Mrs. Morris' funeral with us?"

"What do you do at a funeral?" asked Jeremy.

"We will thank God that he sent Jesus to die for us," said his father. "We will say there is nothing wrong with dying because Jesus makes us live again."

"I want to go with you, Daddy," said Jeremy.

Some questions

Do you know anyone who has died?
Can you talk to someone about death?
What do you want to know about death?

A prayer

Jesus, help me tell my family about my faith so they will know I will be with you when I die. And help me hear my family members tell about their faith so I will know they will be with you when they die. Amen.

One Problem + Two Problems =

1 John 1:8-9

The Harris family was very sad. The manager of the toy store in the shopping center had called to say that Mike had stolen a toy. Mr. Harris went to talk to the manager. The manager told him what Mike had done.

A clerk in the store had seen Mike take the toy. She asked

him to give it back. Mike said he did not have the toy. He yelled at her and ran out of the store. When the manager ran after him, he saw a policeman in the parking lot, and he asked him to bring Mike back in. Mike had the toy in his pocket.

When Mike and his father got home, they went to Mike's room for a talk.

"We have a lot to talk about, son," his father said. "First, do you see that you have made one problem into many problems?"

"I don't know what you mean," said Mike.

"You stole something from the store," said Mr. Harris. "That is the first problem. We have to help you learn that when you stole the toy, you hurt yourself more than you hurt the store."

"I know that now," said Mike.

"If you had given the toy back when the clerk asked for it, we would have had only one problem to work on," said his father. "But you lied to the clerk as well. That makes two problems. Then you ran out of the store and the police had to bring you back. That's three problems."

Mike was quiet for a long time. Finally he said, "I'm sorry I did all those things, Dad."

"And I forgive you, Mike," his father said. "You and I both know that Jesus died to forgive our sins. What you did was a crime and you may have to go to court. But the sin is forgiven by God."

"Are you mad at me?" asked Mike.

"I was," said his father. "Now I am hurting for you instead of being mad at you. I want you to learn something from this so that neither of us will be hurt again."

"I won't steal anymore. Honest!" Mike said.

"I believe you, son, but you can learn more than that," his father said.

"I think I have learned not to make one problem into three problems," said Mike.

"Today has been a sad day for us," said Mr. Harris. "But I think you've made something good come out of it. It's easier to get rid of little problems before they grow into big ones."

"Thanks, Dad! You helped me."

"I love you, son."

Some questions

Have you ever made one problem into many problems?

Why should you admit it when you have done something wrong?

Do you know how to ask for forgiveness?

A prayer

Dear God, forgive me when I do what is wrong, and help me do what is right. In Jesus' name. Amen.

A Stranger at the Playground
Ephesians 6:10-13

"Do you want something to eat?" Willie's mother asked when he came home from playing.

"No, I'm not hungry," said Willie.

"What's wrong with you?" asked his mother. "You're always hungry after you've been at the playground."

"I just ate a big candy bar," he answered.

"Where did you get money to buy that?" his mother asked.

"I had a dollar. See, I've got some left," he said as he showed his mother some coins.

"Where did you get the dollar?" she asked.

"A nice man gave it to me at the playground."

"What is his name?" asked his mother.

"I don't know his name," said Willie.

"Why would someone you don't know give you a dollar?"

"I don't know," Willie said. "Maybe he's a Christian, like us."

"Christians do help other people," said his mother, "but you didn't need the dollar."

"Maybe he thought I did," said Willie.

"You are a friendly boy, Willie, and I'm glad," his mother said. "People like you, and we want you to like people."

"I learned in Sunday school that Jesus loves everyone, and we can love everyone too," said Willie.

"I'm glad you learned that," said his mother. "But we have to learn to love people in the right way."

"How?" asked Willie.

"Some people know you well," said his mother. "They talk to you. They hug you. They give you presents."

"Like you and Daddy, and Grandma, and Uncle Art and Aunt Gladys, and the pastor, and my Sunday school teacher?"

"Yes, they are your friends," said his mother. "Then there are other people who talk to you. But they do not hug you. They don't give you presents."

"Like Mrs. Ellis next door," said Willie, "and Jimmy's mother, and the man who brings the mail."

"Right!" said his mother. "There are many people like that whom you know. You might talk to them when others are around. But you don't let them touch you, and they don't give you presents."

"Like the man at the playground?" asked Willie.

"Yes," said his mother. "Like the man at the playground. If a stranger gives you a present, asks you to get in a car, or wants to touch you, always say no and run away very fast."

"But what if he is a nice person who wants to be my friend?" asked Willie.

"The person at the playground may be a nice person. And he may eventually become your friend," said his mother. "But a nice person will understand that you have to be careful about strangers. He will talk to you when another adult is around, and he will tell you who he is."

"Do I have to give the dollar back?" asked Willie. "I spent most of it."

"No," his mother said. "But if you see the man again, ask the supervisor at the playground to find out who he is."

"OK," said Willie. "Maybe I *will* have something to eat."

Some questions

What places in your neighborhood should you avoid unless an adult is with you?

What should you do if a stranger offers you a gift or a ride in a car?

A prayer

Dear God, protect all children from people who would hurt them. In Jesus' name. Amen.

I Don't Have Anything to Do
Luke 14:12-14

"Can I watch TV?" Mark asked for the third time as he followed his mother to the kitchen on a Saturday afternoon.

"No, there's nothing on television for you to watch now," said his mother. "Why don't you read a book?"

"I'm tired of reading," complained Mark.

"Then play a game or get out some of your toys," suggested his mother.

"I don't have anyone to play with," said Mark.

"Then phone someone," said his mother. "You know you can invite a friend over any time you want."

"I don't have any friends," said Mark. "No one likes me."

Mark's mother stopped her work. She looked worried.

"Mark, you know how your family loves you. You know Jesus loves you. You do have friends."

"But you don't count," said Mark. "Your family *has* to love you. And Jesus loves everyone. But I don't have any other friends."

"Do you know how to make a friend?" asked Mark's mother.

"I phoned Jimmy. He has lots of friends. They all went to the park together," said Mark. "And Brian had a birthday party. He didn't invite me."

"Do all the boys and girls in your class have lots of friends?" asked his mother.

"No," said Mark. "But Brian and Jimmy do."

"Who doesn't have any friends?" his mother asked.

"I don't," Mark said.

"Anyone else?" asked his mother.

"Joey's all alone because he has thick glasses and can't play well," said Mark. "And no one talks to Sara because she doesn't talk to anyone. And Jason's fat. He doesn't have many friends."

"What do you think Joey, Sara, and Jason are doing now?" asked Mark's mother.

"Nothing," said Mark.

"Then why don't you invite them over?" she asked.

"But they don't do anything," Mark said. "They aren't fun like Jimmy and Brian."

"Maybe they could do something if you showed them how," said Mark's mother. "They might be able to teach you something too."

"Joey plays chess," said Mark. "And Sara has lots of music on tapes. Jason reads lots of books."

"I think it would be fun to have them here," his mother said. "Maybe you've learned something about making friends."

"What?" asked Mark.

"When you want a friend, find someone who also needs a friend," said his mother. "Go and phone them. I'll make some popcorn."

Some questions

How do you choose your friends?

Do you ever choose a friend who needs a friend?

When you are lonely, can you find another lonely person?

A prayer

Jesus, thank you for loving me even when I don't feel lovable. Help me to love others. Amen.

It Isn't Fair!
1 Corinthians 13:4-7

"No, I won't!" yelled Benji when his mother asked him to clear the table after dinner. "It's Nicole's turn. She never does her share."

"Benji!" his mother said. "I told you to take the dishes off the table, and I want you to do it right now."

"That's not fair!" said Benji. "It's not my turn."

"We will talk about it later, Benji," said his mother. "You do what I've told you to do. After we both calm down we'll talk about it again."

Benji took the dishes from the table to the sink. Tears were in his eyes, but he pretended he was not crying. He dumped the dishes into the sink with a bang. The sound was so loud that he was afraid some of the dishes may have broken. But they hadn't.

When Benji finished with the dishes, he went to his room and turned on his radio very loud. He tried to play with his toys, but it was no fun.

"Now can we have a talk?" asked his mother as she came into the room. Benji didn't say anything for a while. He was still angry. But he knew his mother expected him to talk to her, so he turned the radio off.

"First of all, Benji," said his mother. "I agree that it was not fair for you to have to clear the table. It *was* Nicole's turn."

"Then why did I have to do it?" he asked.

"Because Nicole was invited to a birthday party," his mother said. "She had to get ready to leave."

"But that's not fair!" said Benji.

"Maybe it's not fair," his mother said, "but it is love. I don't think I can always be fair, giving each of you exactly the same things and expecting you to do exactly the same things. But I can—and I do—love you both just the same."

"But she went to a party and I had to do her chores."

"Yes, that's what happened this time," said his mother. "But at other times Nicole helps you. Daddy and I want to be fair, but we know life is not always fair. Even when things aren't fair, we want you to know we still love you."

"If you love me, you'll be fair," said Benji.

"Yes, we'll try," his mother said. "But if we were only doing what was fair, we wouldn't do nearly as much for you as we do. When we try to be fair, we only do what we *have to* do. When we love you, we do all we *can* do. Do you like that better?"

"Yes," said Benji.

"I'm glad you understand," said his mother. "When something happens that you think is not fair, I want you to remember all the times you got more than what was fair. That helps a lot."

"I'll try," said Benji.

"Fine!" said his mother as she turned on his radio. "And next time, don't throw down the dishes!"

Some questions

Will other people always be fair with you?

Will you always be fair with others?

What should you do when others are unfair with you? When you are unfair with others?

A prayer

Dear Jesus, forgive me when I am unfair to others and help me forgive those who are not fair to me. Amen.

A Visit to the Hospital
Matthew 25:34-40

Daymon sat in the hospital waiting room as he waited for his father to park the car. This was his first time in a hospital. He was going to see his mother. She had been operated on the day before. He had been worried about his mother. His daddy had said she would get well, and they had prayed for her together.

When Daymon's father came in, they got on the elevator and went up to the fifth floor. Then they walked down the hall to room 514. Daymon almost didn't recognize his mother when he saw her. She looked tired and lonely. He was not used to seeing her in bed.

"Hi, Daymon," she said, "I'm glad you came to see me." When Daymon came close to the bed, he knew why he felt funny: everything was backwards. Usually *he* was the one who was sick in bed and his mother would come to see him. This time he had come to see his mother in bed. His mother usually brought presents to *him*. This time he and his father had bought flowers for her.

At first Daymon didn't know what to do in the hospital room. Then he decided to do what his mother had done when she helped him. First he got his mother a drink of water. Then he helped her fix the pillows and blanket. He even asked her where she would like him to put the flowers. Daymon enjoyed being with his mother. He could tell that she was glad he was there.

When his father said they had to go, he gave his mother a big hug and a kiss. Then he remembered that when his mother put him to bed, she always said a prayer with him.

"Would you like me to pray with you?" he asked his mother.

"Yes," his mother said, "I'd like that very much."

"Dear Jesus," said Daymon as he held his mother's hand, "please make my mother well again. Thank you for the doctors and the nurses and this hospital. Bless all the other people who are sick, too. Amen."

Some questions

Have you ever visited anyone in the hospital?

If you were in the hospital, would you want someone to visit you?

Do you know anyone who is ill now?

A prayer:

Dear Jesus, thank you for doctors and nurses and hospitals. Bless everyone who is ill (especially _____). Amen.

God Didn't Do Anything
Matthew 7:7-12

"Wes, you must be tired tonight," said his father as he tucked him in bed. "You don't have much to say."

"I guess not," said Wes.

"Is something bothering you?" his father asked.

"Yes," Wes answered.

"Can you tell me about it?" asked his father.

"No," Wes said.

"Did you talk to God about it?" his father asked.

"Yes," said Wes, "and he didn't do a thing!"

"Maybe you haven't given him enough time," said his father.

"Yesterday I asked him to help," said Wes, "and the day before."

"Once I prayed for something for a long time," his father said. "I thought God didn't hear my prayers. But he did; I got what I prayed for 10 years later."

"God had better not think that I'll wait that long," said Wes.

"Ten years seems like a long time to you," said his father. "That's longer than you have lived. But now I'm glad God took his time in answering my prayer. I needed to get ready for the blessings he gave me."

"I'm ready right now," said Wes.

"I thought I was too," his father said. "Look at it this way: You've got a long life to live. Many good and fun things will happen to you. You've got a lot to look forward to."

"But I want God to help me now," Wes said.

"He does help you now," said his father. "Jesus loves you and is with you. God has given you a family that loves you. You have a good school and you are learning a lot."

"But that's not what I asked for," said Wes.

"But God doesn't give you everything you ask for as soon as you pray for it," his father said. "God knows what is best for you. Sometimes you ask me for things that I don't give you because I know you're not ready for them yet. Because I love you, I won't give you something that might hurt you."

"You mean I shouldn't ask God for what I want anymore?" asked Wes.

"Of course you should," said his father. "Ask him for anything. But remember, God loves you and will help you in the right way."

"OK," said Wes. "Good night, Dad! I want to say my prayers by myself tonight."

"Fine, Wes," said his father. "Good night!"

Some questions

If you don't get what you pray for, does it mean God didn't hear your prayer? Does it mean God doesn't love you?

Would God give you anything that would hurt you?

Is prayer telling God what to do, or is it asking God to do something?

A prayer

Thank you, Jesus, for inviting us to pray to you. I have something special to ask from you now: (include your own prayer). Amen.

We Can't Afford It
Luke 12:22-31

"Hi, Mom," said Sara as she ran into the house. "You know what? I rode Sharon's bicycle today. It's a two-wheeler. And it didn't have training wheels, either."

"That's great, Sara," said her mother. "I hope you didn't fall and get hurt."

"I had a little fall once, but I wasn't hurt," said Sara. "Riding a bicycle is fun!"

Sara found a banana and started eating it. She hoped her mother would ask more about the bicycle. But her mother was busy preparing dinner.

"My birthday is next month," said Sara.

"Yes, I remember," said her mother. "We never forget your birthday."

"What are you going to give me?" Sara asked.

"Daddy and I will talk about that soon," her mother answered.

"I'd like a bicycle like Sharon's," said Sara.

"We'll get you a nice present," said her mother. "But I don't want you to be disappointed on your birthday, so you should know that we can't afford a bicycle."

"But Sharon has one," said Sara. "And so do Chris and Bobby. Everyone in my class has a bicycle."

"Each family has its own money to spend," said her mother. "Some have more money than others. And some families spend it on different things. We can't afford a bicycle."

"Why not?" said Sara, as tears came to her eyes.

"We have had lots of other expenses," her mother said.

"Don't you love me as much as Sharon's parents love her?" asked Sara.

"Of course we do," said her mother. "The amount of money we spend on a gift for you does not show how much we love you. We give you many other things to show our love."

"But I want a bicycle," said Sara, "not other things."

"I know the bicycle is important to you since you don't have one," said her mother. "But other things are important too."

"What things?" asked Sara.

"The time your daddy and I spend with you is important," her mother said. "We listen to you and talk to you. And we see that you have good food. We take you to church and Sunday school so that you can learn about Jesus. We help you with your schoolwork. And you have some toys, too."

"I know all that," said Sara. "But I want a bicycle."

"It's all right for you to want a bicycle," said her mother, "but don't think that a bicycle will make you happy or that without one you will be sad. Some day you will have one. But until then, please enjoy what you do have."

"I'll try," said Sara. "But I'm going to tell Sharon I'll help her with her homework if she'll let me ride hers."

Some questions

Do you know the difference between what you want and what you need?

Is it better to buy the things you need before the things you want?

Is there someone you know who would feel good if you shared something you own with them?

A prayer

Thank you, God, for all that we have. Help us to be satisfied with what you give us and to spend our money for the good of everyone in our family. In Jesus' name. Amen.

It's OK to Be Afraid
John 20:19-23

Billy, Scott, and Adam were walking home from the football game. They were tired, and they wanted to get home and have something to eat.

"I know a shortcut," said Scott. "Let's go this way." He jumped across a ditch and ran toward a tall fence.

"There's a big fence that way," said Billy. "We've got to go around it."

"I know where there's a hole under the fence," said Scott. "We can crawl through it."

"Look at that sign," said Adam. "It says: 'KEEP OUT—HIGH VOLTAGE.' "

"What's *voltage?*" asked Billy.

"That's electricity," said Adam.

"Come on!" said Scott. "The hole is over here."

"I'm not going that way," said Adam.

"You're chicken!" said Scott. "Only sissies get scared."

"Yeah, I'm scared of electricity," said Adam. "And my dad says there's nothing wrong with being scared."

"Well, my dad tells me not to be scared," said Scott.

"I think it's dumb not to be scared of some things," said Adam.

"You're a sissy," said Scott. "I'm not scared of anything."

"Well, I'm scared to run out on the street when there are lots of cars," said Adam. "And I'm scared of big dogs that bite. And I'm scared of strangers who ask me to ride in their cars."

"I'm scared of those things too," said Billy. "Do you think I'm a sissy?"

"No," said Scott. "Sissies are scared of everything."

"I'm not scared of everything," said Adam. "I know Jesus is with me, so I'm not afraid of the dark, and I'm not scared to be alone. And I'm not scared to go on a roller coaster."

"I'm hungry," said Billy. "Let's go home one way or the other."

"OK, we'll go your way," said Scott. "But I'm not scared to jump that ditch."

The three boys jumped back over the ditch and ran home.

Some questions

What are some things you should be scared of?

What are some things you should not be afraid of?

Should you do something dangerous just to prove that you are not afraid?

A prayer

Thank you, God, for protecting us from danger. Guide us so that we will not do dangerous things. In Jesus' name. Amen.

Waiting
Psalm 130:5-7

"Laura," called her mother. "I told you to put the silverware on the table 15 minutes ago."

"In a minute, Mom," Laura answered.

"What are you doing?" her mother asked.

"I'm waiting for Dad to come," she answered.

"Your father will be home in a little while," said her mother.

"He's 10 minutes late already," said Laura.

"You know that he is often late," her mother said. "Traffic is probably heavy today."

"Maybe he had an accident," said Laura.

"Why do you say that?" asked her mother as she turned and noticed tears on her daughter's cheeks.

"Uncle Art got hurt in his car," said Laura. "And Sharon said her grandma died in a car crash. Maybe Daddy will get killed too."

Laura's mother sat down beside her. She held her daughter close to her. "Is that why you are always waiting at the door when I come home?" she asked.

"I'm always afraid you will die in a car crash," said Laura.

"I'm glad you told me," said her mother, "because I don't want you to worry every time you have to wait."

"I always think of accidents when you or Daddy are late," said Laura.

"Car accidents do happen," said her mother. "But almost always we are late for other reasons. Do you remember why I was late yesterday?"

"You had to stop for gas," Laura said.

"Yes," said her mother, "and why was Daddy late last week?"

"Because he had to work late," said Laura.

"And once he was late because he had to take Bob home," her mother said. "And many times he has been delayed in traffic jams."

"I thought he was in an accident every time," said Laura.

"Now I know why you have a hard time waiting," said her mother. "Let me teach you how to wait for us to come home."

"How?" Laura asked.

"First, when a worry comes to your mind, ask God to help," said her mother. "After you pray, think about the many times God has answered your prayers and Daddy has come home on time. Then get busy and put the silverware on the table."

"OK," said Laura. "Dear Jesus, protect Daddy, and bring him home safe. Amen."

"Now the silverware!" said her mother.

Some questions

Does anyone in your family worry if someone else is late?

Does it help if the one who is late phones?

Do you remember when you worried about things that did not happen?

A prayer

Dear God, give me faith so that I do not worry, and also help me remember to pray for your protection. In Jesus' name. Amen.

I Heard You Yelling
Ephesians 4:26-27

Dan got in the car with his father. They were going to get a haircut.

"You're mad at Mom, aren't you?" Dan said to his father as they backed out of the driveway.

"Why do you ask that?" his father asked.

"I heard you yelling at her," said Dan.

"What else did you hear?" asked his father.

"I heard her yelling at you," Dan said. "So I guess she's mad at you too."

"I don't think we were yelling at each other," said his father. "We were speaking loudly."

"When I talk as loud as that," said Dan, "you call it yelling."

"All right," said his father. "We were yelling at each other."

"Are you mad at Mom?" asked Dan.

"Yes, I'm angry at your mother, and she is angry at me right now. Maybe it's good you heard us yell at each other; now you realize that families have to work out problems."

"I don't like you and Mom to be mad at each other."

"I understand that, son," said his father. "But do you know that I also love your mother very much? And I also know that she loves me very much."

"Then why did you yell at each other?" Dan asked.

"Because we disagreed about something," said his father. "I hope you know that your mother and I agree about many more things than we disagree about. Today you heard us when we were angry. Have you also seen and heard us when we are happy together?"

"Sure!" Dan said. "I see you hugging and all that silly stuff lots of times."

"Then I'm glad you heard us arguing today," his father said. "Now you know we can disagree and still love each other."

"The same as when you yell at me," said Dan.

"Yes, I do yell at you sometimes, and yet I still love you a lot," said his father.

"And I love you too, Dad," said Dan. "And I love Mom too."

"I think we both had better tell her that when we get home, don't you think?" said his father.

Some questions

Do you worry if people in your family are angry at one another?

Can someone who is angry at you still love you?

Should people who are angry at one another still talk to each other?

A prayer

Dear Jesus, help me talk to people with whom I am angry, and help me listen to people who are angry with me. Amen.

Thanks for the Help
Galatians 6:2

The Barker family took a long trip. They stopped for a picnic lunch in a large park. They were all tired of sitting in the car, so they ate their lunch as they walked around and looked at the park.

Mrs. Barker took the baby over to the swings. Mr. Barker looked for wild berries. Amy and Alan took some bread to feed the ducks who were swimming on the lake.

Suddenly Amy screamed!

Both parents looked toward the lake and saw Alan struggling in the water. As they both ran over they saw him go under the water and then reach up again. Then Amy reached out, grabbed his hand, and pulled him up on the bank.

Alan was soaking wet, but safe.

"What happened?" his father asked.

"We were just feeding the ducks," said Amy. "And Alan fell in the water."

"I didn't think it would be so deep by the bank," said Alan. He was shaking, not only because he was wet and cold, but also because he realized what could have happened to him.

The rest of the family rushed Alan back to the car. Soon he was dry, and everyone knew he would be OK.

"I want to thank God for saving me," said Alan.

"We all do, Alan," said his mother. "Will you say the prayer?"

"Dear Jesus," said Alan, "thank you for saving me when I fell in the water."

"Jesus didn't save you," said Amy. "I did."

"Dear Jesus," said Alan, "Thank you for sending Amy to save me when I fell into the water. Amen."

Some questions

Does God answer some of your prayers by sending someone else to help you?

Does God answer other people's prayers by sending you to help them?

If someone else helps you in a way that answers a prayer, whom should you thank: God, or the person who helped you?

A prayer

Thank you, God, for sending many people to help me. And send me to help others too. In Jesus' name. Amen.

I Only Asked for a Single
Hebrews 10:35-36

The first year Dirk played Little League baseball he was the youngest player on the team. When he got to play in a real game he was always in right field. Very few balls were knocked to right field. When one did come his way, Dirk seldom caught it.

When Dirk got to bat, he almost never hit the ball. When he did hit it, someone always caught the ball and put him out.

"Dad," said Dirk as they walked home from a game, "I learned a Bible verse in Sunday school that is not true."

"Which verse, son?" his father asked.

"Jesus said, 'Ask and it will be given to you; seek and you will find; knock and the door will be opened to you' [Matthew 7:7]," quoted Dirk. "But when I prayed that I would hit the ball, I didn't get what I asked for."

"I'm glad you prayed for help," said his father. "Maybe God has a different way of answering your prayer."

"But I don't want a different answer," said Dirk. "I want to make a run. And I asked."

"Don't quit praying just because God doesn't answer the first time," his father said. "I still believe what Jesus said."

Dirk and his father talked about prayer several times during the year as the boy continued to play ball—and became a much better player.

Three years later Dirk was one of the older members of the team. He was one of the team's pitchers. At the first game of the season, all of the teams were there. The seats were filled with parents and friends.

When Dirk got up to bat, the bases were loaded. He missed the first pitch. But he hit the second and he hit it hard. It was a home run!

The coach gave the ball that he had hit to Dirk. All his teammates had signed it. As he and his father walked home, Dirk said, "Dad, I only asked him for a single."

Some questions

Have you ever asked God for something that you did not receive?

Have you ever asked God for something and received more than you asked for?

Does God answer some prayers in ways you don't expect?

A prayer

Thank you, God, for listening to all my prayers. Help me keep my eyes and ears open so I can see and hear the way you answer my prayers. In Jesus' name. Amen.

Dad Didn't Help Me!
Matthew 12:33-37

Paul's mother found him crying in his room. She knew he had had a bad day. Paul's teacher had phoned and asked one of his parents to visit the classroom after school. His father had gone to see the teacher with Paul.

"I know you've already talked to Dad and your teacher," said his mother. "Do you want to talk to me too?"

"No," sobbed Paul. "Dad didn't even try to help me. You won't help me either."

"Of course I'll help you," his mother said, "and I know your dad will help you too."

"He didn't help me," said Paul. "He was on the teacher's side instead of my side."

"Why do you think he was on your teacher's side?" his mother asked.

"He believed her," said Paul, "instead of believing me."

"What did your teacher say that he believed?" asked his mother.

"She said I wrote on the walls in the bathroom," answered Paul.

"Why did she say that?" his mother asked.

"The janitor said he saw me do it," said Paul, "and Jenny and Susie are tattletales too."

"Did you write on the walls?" asked his mother.

"Dad didn't see me do it," Paul said. "He's my father. He should be on my side and believe me."

"Should he believe you even if you told a lie?" his mother asked.

"Yes," said Paul. "He should be on my side."

"But he *is* on your side," said his mother. "He wants to help you."

"If he was on my side, he would believe me," Paul said.

"If your dad helped you do something wrong," his mother said, "he'd be hurting you. He helped you by not believing a lie."

"How did he help me?" asked Paul.

"He helped you learn a lesson," said his mother. "You did something you shouldn't have done. Then you lied to cover up what you did. If your dad had helped you lie, he would have been hurting you."

"Just once wouldn't have hurt," said Paul.

"Yes it would have," said his mother. "Your dad and I want you to learn to tell the truth. If we take your side when you tell a lie, we are teaching you to lie."

"He doesn't really love me," said Paul.

"Yes, he does," his mother said. "He loves you so much that he wants to help you even if it hurts. Did he tell you why he agreed with your teacher?"

"Yes," said Paul. "He said that when I do something wrong, the best thing is to admit it and to ask Jesus to forgive me."

"Do you think that's a good idea?" his mother asked.

"I guess so," said Paul.

"Your dad and I have learned a good lesson from Jesus," said his mother. "Jesus doesn't stop loving us when we sin. But he doesn't defend our sin, either. Instead, Jesus forgives us. And we can forgive each other, too."

Paul was silent for a while. Then he said, "Does Dad still love me even after what I did?"

"Of course he loves you," said his mother. "He loves you so much that he doesn't have to pretend you're perfect."

Some questions

If you help someone else to lie, are you also lying?
Do your friends help you if they help you to lie?
Do you help your friends if you help them to lie?

A prayer

Lord Jesus, help me to be honest in all I say, and give me family and friends who will also help me to be honest. Amen.

Why Aren't We a Family?
Matthew 12:46-50

Greg went with his mother to buy groceries. While they were in the supermarket, they met Greg's friend Jimmy and his parents. They were shopping too.

"Why don't we have a family?" asked Greg when they got back in the car.

"Why, we do have a family," said his mother. "You and I are our family."

"But Jimmy has a mother and a father," said Greg. "Our family doesn't have a father."

"We have a different kind of family," his mother said. "Do you think all families have the same number of people?"

"I don't know," Greg said.

"Look at Uncle Jim and Aunt Jan's family," said his mother.

"They have five children. Do you know many families with five children?"

"No," said Greg. "Jimmy's the only kid in his family. But it doesn't make any difference how many kids you have. A family should have two grown-ups."

"I think it's good for a family to have a mother and father," his mother said. "But not every family has two adults. How many adults are in Laura's family?"

"Her grandma lives with her," Greg said. "So there's three."

"It's not how many people live in a house that makes a family," said his mother. "It's how the people feel about each other and how they treat each other."

"I love you, Mom," said Greg.

"I know you love me, son," his mother said. "I love you too."

"I think you're the best mother in the whole world," said Greg.

"And I think you're the best son in the whole world," said his mother. "Do you know what that makes us?"

"What?" Greg asked.

"The best family in the whole world," his mother said.

"Are we really the best family in the world?" asked Greg.

"We're the best family for us," said his mother, "but Jimmy's family is the best for him, and Uncle Jim and Aunt Jan's is the best for them."

"And Laura's family is the best for her," said Greg.

"Right!" his mother said. "Now can this family go home?"

"As long as this family eats when it gets there," said Greg.

Some questions

How many people are there in your family?

Do you know families that are larger than yours? Families that are smaller?

Some people live alone. Can they still have a family?

A prayer

God, thank you for our family. Help us enjoy each other, and help us enjoy other families too. In Jesus' name. Amen.

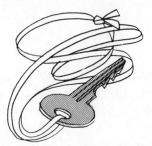

A Latchkey Kid
1 John 4:7-12

"Do you like to be my baby-sitter?" Joshua asked Pam. She was staying with him while his mother went to a meeting.

"Of course I do," answered Pam.

"Do you like me?" asked Joshua.

"Yes," said Pam. "Why do you ask me that?"

"Because some kids don't like me," said Joshua.

"Why do you think they don't like you?" asked Pam.

"They call me a 'latchkey kid,' " Joshua said.

" 'Latchkey kid' isn't a bad name," said Pam. "That doesn't mean they don't like you."

"It *is* a bad name," said Joshua. "It means I have to carry a key to school and go home by myself because no one is home when I get out of school. It means I can't invite anybody to my house after school. It means I can't go to anyone else's house because my mother phones as soon as I get home to see if I'm OK."

"I know what a latchkey kid is," said Pam. "You know, I was a latchkey kid too when I was your age."

"You were?" said Joshua.

"Yes," said Pam. "My father and mother were divorced and I lived with my dad. He was never home when I came home from school."

"Then you know it's a bad name," said Joshua.

"No, I don't think it's a bad name," said Pam. "My father loved me very much, just like your mother loves you. I wish my father and mother had lived together. And I'm sure you wish your parents were together."

"Yes, I do," said Joshua.

"But I figured out that their divorce was not my fault," said Pam. "And your parents' divorce wasn't your fault. Both your mother and father love you. They want to do the best they can for you. And you can help them."

"How?" asked Joshua.

"By loving them," said Pam. "And by showing that you don't feel sorry for yourself. You can have fun when you are living with your mother. Then you can have fun when you go and visit your father."

"But I'm still a latchkey kid," said Joshua.

"You can call yourself that if you want to," said Pam. "I don't think it's a bad name. But I'm going to call you Joshua. I like that name better."

"I do too!" Joshua said.

"Good night, Joshua," said Pam.

"Good night, Pam," said Joshua. "Can I have a drink of water?"

Some questions

Do you know children whose parents are divorced? Has there been a divorce in your family?

Do you know children who get home before their parents do?

Why aren't parents always able to be at home?

A prayer

Jesus, please help all children in families that have had a divorce. Help them to love both parents and to help both parents love them. Amen.

I Need a Dollar
Matthew 25:14-21

Tommy was in a hurry to leave for school. "I need a dollar," he said to his mother as he put on his jacket.

"Why do you need a dollar?" she asked.

"For milk at lunch," he answered.

"You should buy milk from your allowance," said his mother.

"I know," said Tommy. "But I ran out of money this week. I'm in a hurry."

"You should have asked me about this last night," said his mother. "If you've spent all your money, you will have to do without milk today."

"That's not fair, Mom!" said Tommy. "I know you have money in your purse."

"Yes, I have money," she said. "But I have the money because I plan how I spend it. You have to learn how to spend yours. We'll talk about it this evening."

When Tommy came home from school he wanted to go and play in the park. His mother said he could go after they had talked about his allowance.

"Why did you run out of money this week, Tommy?" she asked.

"I bought some candy one day," said Tommy. "And I bought some gum and a kite."

"Why did you buy those things?" his mother asked.

"Because I wanted them," answered Tommy.

"We give you an allowance so you can buy the things you want," said his mother. "But before you buy what you want, you have to buy what you need."

"You tell me that I need milk at school," said Tommy, "but you wouldn't give me any extra money."

"No," said his mother. "We want you to learn how to spend the money we give you. Your allowance is large enough for you to buy the things you need first, and then to use the rest for things you want. If you spend too much on what you want, you can't expect us to give you more money for what you need."

"What if I don't drink milk at school anymore?" asked Tommy.

"Then we will give you less allowance," said his mother. "We want you to learn how to manage your money so you can have both the things you need and things you enjoy."

"OK, but I'm all out of money now," said Tommy.

"You will get your allowance the day after tomorrow," said his mother. "You can do without milk again tomorrow. Next week, buy all the things you need first. Then you can buy other things."

"I'll try," Tommy said. "Do you want to buy me a kite?"

"No," said his mother. "Do you want a glass of milk for free from our refrigerator?"

"Yeah!" said Tommy.

Some questions

Do you think you know how to take care of your money?

Do your parents think you know how to take care of money?

Who could teach you more about spending money the right way?

A prayer

Thank you, Father, for the money I have. Help me to enjoy it and use it wisely. In Jesus' name. Amen.

We Want to Watch That Program
Philippians 4:8-9

"It's time to turn off the TV," Mrs. Jenson told Erica and Roger when the program they were watching was over.

"We want to watch the next show too," said Roger.

"We've got our homework all done," added Erica.

"No, you've seen enough television for one night," said their mother. "Turn it off now."

"Please, Mom," said Erica, "just one more show."

"No," their mother said, "there's nothing on now for you to watch."

"Yes, there is," said Roger. "All the kids watch this show. It's about car crashes and races. It's great!"

112

"It's also about guns and killings," his mother said. "I don't want you to watch it."

"Oh, Mom," said Roger. "It's just a TV show."

Erica and Roger's mother sat down beside them. She picked up the TV program guide and opened it.

"I want to show you two something," she said. "Let's read about the programs that are on TV tonight. Let's think about each one. Let's ask ourselves whether each one is about something that will help us or hurt us."

"This one is about a family that is divorced," said Erica. "The kids live with their mom. Her boyfriend fights with their dad."

"That is a sad story," said their mother. "What if that happened to our family or to one of your friends? Would that be fun to talk about?"

"No," said Erica. "I wouldn't like that."

"Do you know what this one is about?" their mother asked as she pointed to a program on the schedule.

"It's about people who rob a bank and get killed," said Roger. "They've been running ads about it on other shows."

"And this one is about a teenager who uses drugs and dies," their mother said. "This one is about people who kill each other because they are angry and want to get even."

"Are there any good shows on TV?" asked Erica.

"Yes, there are some," said her mother. "We want you to watch programs that help you, not hurt you. We don't want you to see people fight, wreck cars, or kill each other. That's not good entertainment."

"We just watch it for fun," said Roger.

"But it isn't fun," said his mother. "When you see someone die on TV, it looks simple. You don't see the dead person's family and friends. Instead, you see the same actor in another show the next day. It makes it seem as if death isn't real."

"What shows can we watch?" asked Erica.

"You can watch programs that help you understand and enjoy life," said their mother. "Bad things do happen. We want you to see real life. But part of real life is that God loves people, and we also want you to see things that show respect and love for people. We want you to see things that make you feel good about yourselves and others."

"OK," said Roger. "Can we go and play now?"

"That's a good idea!" their mother said.

Some questions

Which programs that you watch on TV seem like real life to you?

Which programs do not show life as it really is?

Do some TV commercials tell you things that are not true?

A prayer

Heavenly Father, help me to learn the difference between what is true and what is not true and between what is real and what isn't. In Jesus' name. Amen.

Helping Someone Who's Sad
James 1:12-15

When Jesse's dad came home from work he looked worried and sad. He sat down in his chair and took his shoes off.

"Are you happy, Daddy?" asked Jesse.

"No, I'm not," said his father. "Things didn't go very well at work today."

"Maybe you need a drink," said Jesse.

"Thanks, son," said his father. "But I'm not thirsty."

"No, I mean a drink to make you feel good," said Jesse.

"Why do you think a drink would make me feel good?" asked his father.

"When Mark's dad comes home tired he says, 'I need a drink,'" Jesse explained. "After he has a drink he's not tired or angry anymore."

"I *am* tired," his father said. "I am also worried, and I may even be angry. But I don't need a drink."

114

"Mark's dad says that drinks make his problems go away," said Jesse.

"No," his father said, "the drinks don't make his problems go away. They just make Mark's father forget his problems for a while."

"Don't you want to forget your problems?" Jesse asked. "Then you'd feel better."

"No," said his father. "I'd rather think about my problems and do something about them. If I try to hide from them by drinking, the problems will get even bigger."

"I don't like you to be worried and sad," said Jesse.

"There's nothing wrong with being worried or sad," said his father, "if it's about something worthwhile. I'm worried about my job because it's a hard job. But I enjoy a hard job. I'm doing something worthwhile. And I get sad when something is wrong in the family. But I'm glad I have a family—even when it makes me sad."

"Can I help you?" asked Jesse.

"Yes," said his father. "You've already helped me by talking to me. I feel better already. And there is something else you could do."

"What?" Jesse asked.

"You could pray for me," his father said.

"OK," said Jesse. "Dear Jesus, thank you for my daddy. Help him do his work. Make him happy. Amen."

Some questions

What do you do when you are worried about something?
Do you think you have to be happy all the time?
Can you help people who are not happy?

A prayer

(Use Jesse's prayer to pray for anyone you know who is unhappy.)

Why Do Grandpa and Grandma Smoke?

Romans 12:1-2

The Bennett family was driving home from a vacation. They were talking about all the fun they had visiting their grandparents on the trip.

"I like staying with Grandpa and Grandma," said Greg. "They do fun things."

"I do too," said Tim. "But why do Grandpa and Grandma smoke cigarettes?"

"Yeah," said Greg, "it made my eyes burn. And they smelled funny when they hugged me."

"Grandpa and Grandma started smoking before they knew how it would hurt their health," said the boys' mother.

"Why don't they give it up?" asked Greg.

"It's not easy for people who have smoked a long time to stop," said their father.

"I know they don't really like smoking," said Tim.

"How do you know?" asked his mother.

"Because Grandpa told me and Greg that he'd give us a hundred dollars when we graduated from high school if we never smoked."

"That shows that he doesn't like smoking," said his father, "because your grandpa always watches his money."

"But I wish he wouldn't have told you that," their mother added.

"Why?" asked Greg. "Do you want us to smoke?"

"No, I hope you never smoke," said his mother. "But there are better reasons for you not to smoke than to please me or to get a hundred dollars from your grandpa."

"What reasons?" asked Tim.

"First of all, for your own health," answered his mother. "God has given you both healthy bodies. Smoke hurts your heart and lungs. We want to help you stay healthy."

"Smoking also takes away some of your energy," said their

father. "People who smoke can't run as far or play sports as well as those who don't."

"I don't want to smoke," said Tim.

"Me either!" said Greg.

"I'm glad about that," said their mother.

"How can we help Grandpa and Grandma to stop smoking?" asked Tim.

"We can't offer them a hundred dollars," said Greg.

"The best way to help is to love them even if they do smoke," said their father. "They love you too, and they will want to do things that help you."

"Maybe our visit will help them stop," said their mother.

"I hope so," said Tim, "because I want them to be there when I graduate from high school."

Some questions

Which is easier, to stop smoking or not to start smoking?

Do you know about the dangers of smoking?

How can you help people who do smoke?

A prayer

Dear God, help us to take care of our bodies. Help those who smoke to stop, and help those who do not smoke so that they do not start. In Jesus' name. Amen.

A New Kid in Class
1 John 2:9-11

"What happened in school today?" Jeremy's mother asked as she gave him a peanut butter sandwich.

"Nothing much," answered Jeremy. "We got a new kid in class. He's a porker."

"What do you mean by that?" asked his mother.

"I mean he's fat," said Jeremy, "as in *real* fat."

"What is his name?" his mother asked.

117

"I don't know," said Jeremy. "Everyone called him 'Tubby.' "

"Would you like to be called that?" asked his mother.

"No," said Jeremy, "but I'm not fat."

"Why do you think the new boy is fat and you aren't?" his mother asked.

"He eats too much," said Jeremy, "and I don't."

"That's probably right," said his mother. "But why does he eat too much, and why do you eat the right amount?"

Jeremy thought a while. "I don't know," he said. "Maybe because his mother is a better cook."

"No, that's not the reason," said his mother. "Do you think that calling him 'Tubby' will make him eat less?"

"Maybe," said Jeremy.

"No, it won't," said his mother. "In fact, it may make him feel bad and cause him to eat more."

"Then he'll get even fatter," said Jeremy.

"When people worry about food all the time, they either eat more and get fat," his mother said, "or they don't eat enough and get too thin."

"Karen is skinny," said Jeremy.

"Yes," said his mother. "I know Karen's mother. She is worried about Karen. Karen thinks she is fat, and she won't eat the right foods."

"But she is skinny," said Jeremy.

"Yes, she is," his mother said. "But she worries about being fat because she hears people talking about it all the time."

"And because she sees people like Tubby," added Jeremy.

"No," said his mother. "It's because she hears people call other people names like 'Fatty' and 'Tubby.' We talk too much about how much people weigh."

"We're talking about it now," said Jeremy.

"I hope our talk is helping you see people in a different way," his mother said. "There are lots of more important things about people than how much they weigh."

"But being fat isn't good for you," said Jeremy.

"That's right!" said his mother. "But the best way to help people with a weight problem is to help them feel good about

118

themselves. Then they don't have to worry about being too heavy or too thin."

"OK," said Jeremy. "I guess this isn't a good time to ask for a piece of cake."

"You're right!" said his mother. "Want an apple?"

Some questions

Has anyone ever called you a name that made you feel bad?

Do you call others names that make them feel bad?

Do you help people change when you call them bad names?

What is the best way to help people feel good about themselves?

A prayer

Dear Jesus, help me to see the good in others and help others to see the good in me. Help us to know that we belong to you and that you love us. Amen.

I Can't Talk about It
1 Corinthians 6:19-20

Connie's mother waited until everyone in the family was out of the house except herself and Connie.

"Let's sit down for a talk," said her mother.

"I'd rather go back to my room and play with my doll," said Connie.

"I'm glad you like your doll," said her mother. "Tell you what: I'll come with you, and then you can hold your doll while we talk." They went to Connie's bedroom together. Connie held her doll and curled up on the bed. Her mother sat down beside her.

119

"I've noticed that you have been sad lately," said her mother. "Is something bothering you?"

"I don't want to talk about it," said Connie.

"I understand that some things are hard to talk about," her mother said. "But I think you can learn to talk about anything."

"I don't want to," said Connie.

"If you had never talked about letters and words, you would never have learned to read," said her mother. "Some people never learn to talk about other things when they are little. When they grow up, they still can't talk about those things."

"But why should I talk about something that makes me feel bad?" asked Connie.

"Because if we talk about it, you can understand it better," said her mother. "Also, I may be able to help you or to find someone else who can help."

"Some of the kids at school say dirty words," said Connie, "and they want me to say them too."

"I'm glad you don't want to say the dirty words, Connie," said her mother. "That's not something that Jesus likes to hear you say. But I want you to know that I love you even if you have said some of those words. Maybe I can help you find good words to say instead of the bad ones."

"Some of the kids want to touch me when they say those words," said Connie.

"Do they want to touch you in private places where you don't want to be touched?" asked her mother.

"Yes," said Connie as tears ran down her cheeks. Her mother reached out her arms, and Connie crawled on her lap.

"I'm so glad we can talk about this, Connie," said her mother. "You don't have to feel bad about yourself. Your body is good and beautiful. Is there something we can do to stop others from doing that to you?"

"Do I have to go to Betsy's house anymore?" asked Connie.

"No," her mother said. "You don't ever have to go there again."

"But I have to go to the bathroom at school sometimes," said Connie.

"Yes, you do," said her mother. "But I can talk to the teacher about that, so it will not be a problem for you."

"Would you?" asked Connie.

"Sure I would," said her mother. "I'm glad we talked about this. I bet we can talk about anything from now on."

"I hope so," said Connie. "Thanks, Mom, I feel better."

Some questions

Do other children talk about things that you would like to ask adults about?

Are there some things you can't talk about because you don't know the right words?

Is there something special you'd like to talk about now?

A prayer

Dear God, when I have problems, help me to talk to other people—and to you. In Jesus' name. Amen.

I'm Sorry, Son
Ephesians 6:4

Everything had gone wrong that day. Tommy had gotten into trouble in the lunchroom at school. When he came home, his mother was angry at him because he had left his clothes on the floor in the bathroom. But the worst thing of all happened at the dinner table.

When Tommy's father heard about what happened at school and about the clothes in the bathroom, he warned Tommy that if he caused any more problems, he would be punished. Tommy felt bad and didn't want to eat. When no one was looking he gave some of his food to his cat under the table. When the cat wanted more food, Tommy couldn't give it any more because his father was watching. So the cat jumped on the table.

Tommy's father got very angry and yelled at him. He said Tommy was a bad boy who always caused problems for his family. Then Tommy was sent to his room, and began to cry. He decided that he must be a bad person because everyone was angry at him.

Then Tommy heard a knock on his door. His father said, "Tommy, may I come in?"

"Yes," said Tommy.

His father came into the room and sat down beside him. He said, "I know you had a bad day, Tommy. So did I. I know I added to the problems you already had. I'm sorry, son."

Tommy was surprised. He thought his father had come to his room to punish him. "I'm sorry I'm a bad boy," said Tommy. "I don't want to cause problems."

"You're not a bad boy," said his father. "You are a good son to me, and I love you. I look forward to coming home from work so I can be with you."

"But I made you angry tonight," said Tommy.

"No," his father said, "I let myself get angry. Because I love you, I feel hurt when you get into trouble at school or at home. I want to help you so that you feel good when you are with other people."

Tommy crawled up on his father's lap. He felt good again. His father did not look angry anymore.

"Do you remember what we say together in church when we confess our sins to God?" asked his father. "We ask Jesus to forgive us. Then the pastor tells us that Jesus died for us and that's why God forgives us. I forgive you for the things you did wrong today, Tommy. Will you forgive me?"

"Yes," said Tommy. "And I'll do better tomorrow."

"So will I," said his father.

Some questions

Do mothers and fathers ever make mistakes?
Can children forgive and help their parents?
Can parents forgive and help their children?

A prayer

Dear Jesus, thank you for forgiving us. Please help us to forgive one another. Amen.

122

My Cat Died!

Matthew 5:1-4

Amy liked to get to school early. She knew her best friend Jackie would always be there. The two friends liked to play on the swings. Sometimes they helped their teacher. But most of all they liked to talk to each other.

One morning Jackie wasn't there. At least she wasn't on the playground or in the classroom. Then Amy found her sitting on the front steps by herself.

"Hi, Jackie," called Amy. "Let's go swing!"

"I don't want to," said Jackie.

"Why not?" Amy asked.

"My cat died," said Jackie as tears ran down her face.

Amy felt sad. She was sad because her friend was sad. And she was sad because she had liked Jackie's cat too.

"What happened?" asked Amy.

"I don't know," said Jackie. "When I got home, Mom said she had taken Mitzy to the vet. But it was too late. Mitzy died."

"You can come to my house after school," said Amy. "I'll let you play with my dog."

"No, thanks," Jackie said. "Your dog is OK, but I want Mitzy."

"Can you get another cat?" Amy asked.

"Mom said we will get another one," said Jackie. "But I don't want another one—I want Mitzy!"

"I think you're lucky that you can get another cat," said Amy. "Carol can't have a cat because her brother is allergic to cats. And my cousins can't have cats because they live in an apartment where they can't keep pets."

"But another cat wouldn't be as nice as Mitzy," Jackie said.

"How do you know?" Amy asked. "If you had had another cat first, you wouldn't have found out how nice Mitzy was. I liked Mitzy, but I like other cats too."

"But I had Mitzy for a long time," said Jackie, "ever since I can remember."

"And you can always remember her," said Amy. "But you can get another cat, and you can do other things."

"Will you help me find a name for another cat?" asked Jackie.

"Sure!" said Amy. "Now let's go swing before the other kids get here."

Some questions

Has something bad ever happened to one of your pets that made you sad? Did you let someone help you?

How could you help a friend who was sad because something bad happened to a pet?

Can you learn something good from a sad experience?

A prayer

Father in heaven, thank you for animals, for my pets, and for other people's pets. Help us take good care of them. In Jesus' name. Amen.

Let's All Help Andy
1 Thessalonians 5:14-15

"We have a new student in our class today," said the teacher. "I want you all to meet Andy. Andy, after a while you'll to get to know the names of the other children in our class."

All the others had already noticed Andy. He was handicapped. His legs looked short, and his feet did not point forward. He used a walker to help himself walk. It took him a long time to get down the hall, through the door, and to his desk.

"Let's all help Andy!" said Jason.

"That's a good idea," said the teacher. "In our class we all need to help each other. So each of you can help Andy, and Andy can help each of you."

"But how can he help us?" Jason asked.

"Andy was born with a problem in his legs," said the teacher. "But he has learned to use his walker very well."

"We could help by getting things for him so that he won't have to use the walker," said Nicole.

"Let's find another way," said the teacher. "Andy can take care of himself just as well as you can. He can get whatever he needs."

"But it takes him a long time to go anywhere," said John.

"Maybe it takes him longer to go somewhere than it would take you," said the teacher. "But Andy is in school to learn to take care of himself, just as you all are here to learn how to take care of yourselves."

"Then how can we help Andy?" asked Jason.

"Let's ask Andy to answer that," said the teacher. "How can the other students help you, Andy?"

"They can talk to me and be my friends," said Andy.

"And what can you do for them?" the teacher asked.

"I'll be their friend too," said Andy.

"That sounds good to me!" said the teacher. "Do any of you want to ask Andy anything?"

"What games do you like?" asked Nicole.

"I like to play chess and checkers," Andy said. "But I like to watch soccer and basketball."

"We've got a great soccer team," said Jason. "Will you come and cheer for us?"

"Sure!" said Andy. "And I can keep score if you want me to."

"You can talk about that at recess," said the teacher. "But now it's time for math. Take out your books."

Some questions

Have you heard other children tease someone who was handicapped or different from them?

How can you help a person who is handicapped?

Do you let others help you when you need help?

A prayer

Lord God, help others who have handicaps, and teach us how we can help one another. In Jesus' name. Amen.

You Love Her More Than Me

James 3:13-16

Laura liked her mother to read to her. But just as her mother finished the first page of a good book, Laura's baby sister started crying.

"I'll have to go check on Jenny," said her mother as she put the book down and left Laura on the couch. Laura waited for a long time. Finally her mother returned, carrying the baby.

"Now we can finish the story," said her mother as she sat down beside Laura.

"I don't want you to read to me now," said Laura as she grabbed the book and closed it.

"But that's a good story!" said her mother. "We want to find out what happens."

"I don't want you to read to me while you are holding Jenny," Laura said.

"But Jenny won't bother us now," her mother said. "I changed her, and she is happy again."

"But I want you to read to me—not to her," said Laura. "Before she came you always used to read to me. You don't anymore."

"But I read to you almost every day," said her mother.

"No, you read to the baby," Laura said. "You love her more than me."

"No, Laura," her mother said. "I love you both very much."

"When she cried, you stopped reading to me and went to see her," said Laura.

"Jenny needed help then," said her mother. "So I helped her—like I help you when need me."

"You helped me more before Jenny came," said Laura.

"When you were little, you needed me more, just like Jenny does now," her mother said. "But I don't love you any less.

And now you will get more love, because Jenny can love you too."

"She can't love me," Laura said.

"Yes she can," said her mother. "You learned to love me because I held and loved you when you were Jenny's age. That's why I let you hold her and help—so that you can love her and she can love you."

"But I want to be with you," said Laura.

"And I want to be with you, too," her mother said. "I can love both you and Jenny. I love you just as much as I did before Jenny was born. Now I read to both of you. But you are learning to read. Some day you can read to Jenny."

"Do you think she will like that?" asked Laura.

"Sure she will!" said her mother. "She will be happy to have a big sister who loves her and reads to her. Now, are you ready to get back to that story?"

"OK," said Laura. "Let's start at the beginning."

Some questions

Do your parents or teachers sometimes give more attention to others than to you? Does that mean they love you less?

Are you jealous of someone in your family? Can you talk about your jealousy?

Can Jesus love all other people too without loving you less?

A prayer

Lord Jesus, thank you for loving all of us. Help us to love one another. Amen.

Would God Play with Us?

Psalm 114

Dirk, Tim, and Wes had a favorite summertime game—a water balloon fight. Part of the fun was filling the balloons with water. They would take turns putting a balloon on the tap and turning the water on. Sometimes water would spray out and make them wet. Once in a while a balloon would burst and the water would splash on everyone. After the balloons were filled, they would throw them at one another. When a balloon hit one of the brothers, it would break and splash water everywhere. It was fun on a hot day!

One day they asked their father if they could go outside for a water balloon fight.

"Sure!" their dad said, "but clouds are coming up from the west. I think it will be raining soon."

The boys ran to get in their swimming suits. Then they each started filling their balloons with water. But before they could finish, the rain came down. All three of the boys were soaking wet when they rushed back into the house.

"I can see who won the water balloon fight today," said their father, as he got out towels for them.

"We didn't even get a chance to play," said Dirk.

"It rained too soon," said Tim.

"It looks to me as if God won," said their father. "God soaked all three of you."

"Would God play with us?" asked Dirk.

"Sure he would!" said Wes. "Jesus was a little boy once."

"But they didn't have balloons then," said Tim.

"That doesn't make any difference," said Wes. "He liked to play just like we do."

"I think God could have fun playing with you," said their father. "He said he'd be with you always, so that must include while you are playing."

"God did get us all wet today," said Dirk. "And that was fun."

128

"And we've still got our balloons ready for another game as soon as it stops raining," said Tim.

"But not until we find more dry towels!" said their father.

Some questions

Would you like God to play with you?
What games do you think God would like to play with you?
Is it fun to be with God?

A prayer

Jesus, thank you for living with us. Help us have fun together. Amen.

What Does *Adopted* Mean?
Galatians 4:4-7

"Mom, what does *adopted* mean?" Kevin asked while he was helping his mother cut celery.

"It can mean several things," said his mother. "How did you hear the word used?"

"The kids at school say that Erica was adopted," said Kevin.

"Yes," said his mother. "I know Erica's family. She was adopted."

"What does that mean?" asked Kevin.

"It means that Erica had another mother and father before she came to live with the Clarks," his mother said.

"That means Mr. and Mrs. Clark are not her real parents," said Kevin.

"No, Mr. and Mrs. Clark are her real parents," said his mother. "When they adopted her, they became her parents. She has their names. They take care of her just like your dad and I take care of you."

"But what happened to Erica's first mom and dad?"

"I don't know," said his mother. "There are many reasons why children are adopted. Maybe her first parents died. Maybe there was some health or money reason why they couldn't take care of their child. Maybe they were not married and could not give a baby a home."

"Maybe they didn't love her," said Kevin.

"No, I think they loved her very much," said his mother. "They wanted her to have a good home. The courts always check out new parents before they are allowed to adopt a child. The Clarks give Erica a good home."

"Is it bad to be adopted?" asked Kevin.

"Oh, no!" said his mother. "It is good to be adopted. Erica is glad to live with her mother and father, and they are glad to have her. She is very special for them because they waited a long time for her. They asked God to help them have a baby, and this is the way he answered their prayer."

"I wish I were adopted," said Kevin. "Then I'd know I was very special to you."

"But you *are* very special to Daddy and me," said his mother. "It's not important whether you were adopted or not. It is important that you love your parents and that they love you. Your Daddy and I prayed for a baby—and God gave us *you!*"

"Do adopted kids have to do chores too?" asked Kevin.

"Yes, they do," said his mother. "When you finish with the celery, I want you to set the table."

"OK," said Kevin. "I hope Erica has to set the table too—and wash the dishes."

Some questions

If you were (or if anyone in your family was) adopted, are there questions you'd like to ask about the adoption?

Do you have friends who were adopted? Are you glad that those children have parents, and that the parents have children, through the adoption?

A prayer

Father in heaven, help all children who need parents and all adults who want children, so that adoptions may be a blessing to all of them. Amen.

130

But He's My Friend!

Philippians 1:9-11

When Jimmy came home from school he was crying. He threw his lunchbox down and ran to his room. His mother found him curled up on his bed.

"What's the matter, Jimmy?" she asked.

"I got into a fight with Mike and Sean," said Jimmy. "They're not my friends anymore."

"What caused the fight?" his mother asked.

"They said bad things about Jon," said Jimmy. Jon was the 16-year-old boy who lived next door to Jimmy and his parents. Jon would often play with Jimmy and had taught him to ride a bicycle.

"What did they say about Jon?" asked his mother.

"They said that he smoked pot and that he was arrested because he stole something from the shopping center," Jimmy said. "I know Jon didn't do that because he's my best friend."

"I know Jon is your good friend," said his mother as she pulled Jimmy close to her. "But I talked to Jon's mother today. He *was* arrested at the shopping center yesterday."

"Then the police must have made a mistake!" said Jimmy. "Jon wouldn't steal anything."

"Jon admitted to the police and his parents that he's been stealing things from stores for several months," said his mother sadly.

"Why would he steal anything?" asked Jimmy.

"He told the police he needed the money to buy drugs," said his mother.

"But he's my best friend," sobbed Jimmy. "I want to be like him when I get big."

"Even good friends can do wrong things," said his mother. "When you grow up, you can be like Jon in some ways. You can be friendly and kind. You can help other little boys."

"Is Jon going to go to jail?" asked Jimmy.

"I don't know," said his mother. "Jon did something that hurt many people. He is sorry, and he wants us all to forgive him.

We hope that he has learned a lesson and will not steal or use drugs anymore. Maybe you can learn from Jon's mistake too."

"I'm not going to smoke that dumb stuff," said Jimmy.

"I hope you don't!" said his mother. "I also hope you learn that what you do can either help many people or hurt many people. Jon didn't stop to think that what he was doing would hurt his friends as well as his parents."

"I feel sorry for Jon," said Jimmy. "I hope he can still be my friend."

Some questions

Can someone be a "good person" and a "bad person" at the same time?

Can the things you do make other people happy? sad?

How do you know that you are forgiven after you have done something wrong? How can you forgive a friend who does something wrong?

A prayer

Dear Jesus, help me to be a good friend to others, and help others to be good friends to me. Amen.

Bad Dreams
2 Corinthians 1:3-5

Lisa's father woke up in the middle of the night when he heard a strange sound. He listened carefully and heard Lisa talking. He went quickly to her room.

"No! No!" Lisa was saying. "Go away! Help! Go away!" She was talking in her sleep. Her father could see that she was having a bad dream. He sat down beside her and touched her hand.

"You're OK, Lisa," he said. "I'm here with you."

Lisa woke up and saw her father. She grabbed his hand.

"I'm with you, Lisa," he said. "You were having a bad dream. It's all right now."

"I'm glad you're here, Daddy," she said. "I was all alone and a big bear was about to get me. Then I ran and I fell, and I just kept on falling."

"It was only a dream," said her father.

"But I was scared," she said. "No one was there to help me. I couldn't breathe."

"Do you have this dream often?" her father asked.

"Sometimes," she said. "The bear isn't there all the time. But I always fall and fall."

"Most people have bad dreams sometimes," said her father.

"Does that mean the dream will come true sometime?" asked Lisa. "Will I fall a long way some time? Will a bear chase me?"

"No, dreams don't tell you what is going to happen," said her father. "Dreams are just pretend-ideas. Sometimes we talk about daydreams. Daydreams are pretend-ideas that we think about. Bad dreams are pretend-ideas that happen while we are asleep."

"But I don't want to pretend bad things," said Lisa.

"I know you don't," said her father. "When the bad dream comes, always remember it is only a dream. Don't think about the bad dream when you are going to sleep. Instead think about good things. Say your prayers; then go to sleep with happy thoughts."

"I'll try," said Lisa.

"We'd better both do that right now," said her father. "Good night, Lisa! Sleep tight!"

" 'Night, Daddy!" said Lisa. "Thanks."

Some questions

Do you remember some of your dreams? Were they good dreams or bad dreams?

Do you think it would help if you told someone about your bad dreams?

A prayer

Dear God, help me have a good night's sleep and give me good dreams. In Jesus' name. Amen.

134

Jesus Is a Good Name

Philippians 2:9

Jason was helping his father paint the yard fence. He liked working with his father. He knew he was growing up when he could do things that his father did.

As Jason reached out to put his brush in the can of paint, he knocked the side of the can and tipped it over. The paint ran out into the grass.

"Oh, Jesus!" yelled Jason.

His father quickly grabbed the can and turned it upright. He saved most of the paint. He also put some newspaper on the grass to soak up the spilled paint.

"Don't worry, son," said his father. "Sometimes accidents happen when we work. But why did you say 'Jesus!' when you spilled the paint?"

"I don't know," said Jason.

"It didn't sound like you were praying for help," said his father. "Were you?"

"I guess not," said Jason. "But that's what Uncle Kirk says when something goes wrong."

"Your Uncle Kirk says some other things that I wouldn't say—and that I'd rather you didn't say," his father said.

"What's wrong with saying 'Jesus'?" asked Jason. "*Jesus* is a good word."

"That's right. *Jesus* is a *very* good word," said his father. "Since it's a good word, it should be used in good ways. What are some good ways we say 'Jesus'?"

"When we pray," said Jason, "and when we go to church."

"Right!" his father said. "And we can use the name of Jesus in many other ways. We can talk about him often because he is our friend."

"Then what did I say wrong?" asked Jason.

"You sounded angry to me," said his father. "Since *Jesus* is a good word, we don't use it to show anger or hate."

"I guess I was just mad at myself for spilling the paint," said Jason.

"Maybe so," his father said, "but Jesus isn't mad at you. Maybe you said it because you thought it made you sound big, like Uncle Kirk."

"Maybe," Jason said.

"And maybe we'd better get our painting done," said his father, "or maybe we won't get any lunch."

Some questions

When you use Jesus' name, does it sound as if he loves you and you love him?

Which people do you learn good words from? Which people do you learn bad words from?

Do other people learn good words or bad words from you?

A prayer

Dear Jesus, thank you for being our friend. Help us use your name in the right way. Amen.

I Don't Want to Sleep Alone
Psalm 23

"It's your bedtime, Erica," said her father as he turned off the TV set.

"Can I sleep with you and Mommy tonight?" asked Erica.

"No," said her father, "you have a nice bed in a nice room and that's where you sleep."

"But I don't want to sleep alone," she said. "I'd rather sleep with you."

"You have asked to sleep in our bed every night this week," said her father, "and we have said no every time. Why do you keep on asking?"

"You never tell me why I have to sleep in my own room," she said.

"OK, tonight I'll tell you why," said her father. "One reason is that we want you to have a good night's sleep, and we want to sleep well also. All of us will sleep better in our own beds. Another reason is that your mother and I also want to be by ourselves sometimes."

"But I'm part of the family too," said Erica. "Why can't I be with you?"

"You *are* an important part of our family," said her father. "We both like to have you with us. We both spend time with you. But we also love each other, and sometimes we want to be alone. We still love you when we're not with you, even when you're at school."

"Will you come to my room to say goodnight?" asked Erica.

"Yes," said her father. "And your mother will also give you a goodnight hug and kiss."

"In my room?" asked Erica.

"In your room," her father said. "Let's go!"

Some questions

Do you want to be together with your whole family sometimes?

Are there times when you want to be with only your father or mother?

Do you like to be alone sometimes?

A prayer

Dear God, help me to enjoy being with others, and help me also to enjoy being alone. In Jesus' name. Amen.

David Did It
John 8:31-32

When Mrs. Acker came into the kitchen she saw Tootsie, the family's pet cat, eating from her dish. She knew it was not time for the cat to have food. When she looked closely, she discovered that Tootsie was eating the leftover meat loaf that she had planned to serve for lunch. Mrs. Acker went into the den where the children were watching TV.

"Who gave Tootsie the meat loaf?" she asked.

"David did it!" answered Johnny. Katie and Sarah started laughing because they knew that Johnny had given the meat loaf to Tootsie. They also knew that there was no one named David in their house. David was a 'pretend-friend' that Johnny often talked about.

"You come with me," said Mrs. Acker, as she lead Johnny back to the kitchen. "Now I want to ask you one more time: Who gave the meat loaf to Tootsie?"

"I told you. David did it," said Johnny.

"Johnny, you know David is not a real person," said his mother. "You pretend that you play with David. But that is not real."

"It's real that Tootsie was hungry," Johnny said.

"Tootsie does get hungry and we feed her well," said his mother. "But it was not time for her to eat; and when she does eat, we have cat food for her. The meat loaf was for our lunch."

"I pretended that David fed her," said Johnny.

"You may have pretended that," said his mother, "but you also opened the refrigerator and took out the meat loaf. That was real."

"But I was only helping David," Johnny said.

"No," said his mother, "*you* did it. It is OK to pretend when you play games. But you must always know what is pretend and what is real. Can you tell the difference?"

"Yes," said Johnny. "Tootsie is real. The meat loaf was real."

"That's right," said his mother. "Now what is pretend?"

"David is 'pretend,' " Johnny said.

"Now the important part," said his mother. "Who gave the meat loaf to Tootsie?"

"I did," said Johnny.

"Right!" said his mother. "And who is going to eat a cheese sandwich for lunch while the rest of us eat ham?"

"I think I am," said Johnny.

"Right again!" said his mother.

Some questions

What are some of the things you like to pretend are real?

Do you always know what is pretend and what is real?

Would you like to ask if some things are real or pretend?

A prayer

Lord God, help me to know what is true and what is real, even when I pretend. In Jesus' name. Amen.

I Can't Be Like Sarah
1 Corinthians 12:12-20

It was report card time. Sarah rushed home from school to show her grades to her mother. She had 'A's in every subject. Her teacher had also added a note. It said, "Sarah is a good student and does all her work well."

Sarah's younger sister Katie walked home slowly that day. She came into the house quietly and went to her room.

"Hi, Katie," said her mother as she walked by the room. "I didn't hear you come in. Where's your report card?"

"I'll show it to you later," said Katie.

"Maybe we'd better look at it now," said her mother.

Katie got out her report card and handed it to her mother. It had a couple of 'B's, several 'C's and one 'D'. There was also a note from her teacher. It said, "Katie does not pay attention in class and does not hand in her work on time."

"I can't be like Sarah," said Katie, as tears rolled down her cheek. "She studies all the time, and the teachers always like her. The teachers always tell me I should be like her. But I can't be."

"You don't have to be like Sarah," said her mother. "You are Katie, and you must do as well as Katie can do."

"I don't want to study hard," said Katie, "because I know I'll never get 'A's in everything."

"You don't have to get good grades because of Sarah," said her mother. "I don't even want you to study just to get good grades. But I do want you to pay attention in class and to hand in your assignments on time. When you study and pay attention you learn things. That's the important thing about going to school."

"But I never get it all right," said Katie. "It's too hard."

"If all the lessons were easy, you wouldn't learn anything," said her mother. "You go to school to learn as much as you can. You are not there to do as well as Sarah."

"I know you think Sarah's report card is always better than mine," said Katie.

"Each person has special abilities," said her mother. "Sarah is good in schoolwork. You can play ball better than she can. But Sarah can still play ball and you can still study as hard as you can and do as well as you can."

"Will Daddy be angry about my report card?" asked Katie.

"He and I will talk about it," said her mother. "And we will both help you. We are not angry at you. We love you."

Some questions

Do you think parents and teachers appreciate your brothers, sisters, or friends more than you because they get better grades?

Do you think you are better than someone else because you get higher grades?

What can you do really well? Is there something you cannot do well?

140

Dear God, help me to do well the things I can do so that I can help others. And help others to help me with those things that I can't do as well. In Jesus' name. Amen.

But Yesterday You Said

1 John 2:12

Bethany was eager to get all her Saturday chores done. She cleaned her room and put all the toys away.

"My, you are a good worker today!" said her mother as Bethany emptied her wastebasket.

"I'm almost done," said Bethany. "Then you can take me over to Amy's house."

"Oh, I forgot that you planned to go to Amy's today," said her mother. "I'm sorry, I won't be able to take you."

"But yesterday you said I could go," said Bethany. "You said that if I cleaned my room, you would take me to Amy's house."

"I remember that I promised you that," said her mother. "But I didn't know your daddy would have to work today. He had to take the car, so I have no way to drive you to Amy's."

"But you promised!" said Bethany. "You tell me that I have to keep my promises. And I cleaned the room because I said I would."

"Yes, you did a good job on your room," said her mother. "And I will see that you get to visit Amy soon. But I have no car now, and Daddy will not get home until late tonight."

"It's not fair!" said Bethany as she started to cry.

"I agree that it's not fair," said her mother. "But neither Daddy nor I wanted to hurt you. We love you and like to help you. We are glad that Amy is your friend and that she invites you to her house. But Daddy's job is important for all of us. He had to work today, so we can help him by giving up the car."

"But I told Amy I would be there because you said you would take me. She'll think I don't like her if I don't come."

"We will phone Amy and explain why you can't come," said her mother. "You and I will have a good time at home today. I can't go anywhere either, so we will enjoy each other."

"Can we look at the pictures of you, me, and Daddy when I was a little baby?" asked Bethany.

"Sure we can!" said her mother. "Bethany, I'm glad you can understand that sometimes we can't do the things we want to do. Plans change. But we can still have a good time."

"We'll have fun," said Bethany. "But let's look at the pictures in *your* room—I don't want mine to get messy."

Some questions

Can you keep every promise you make?

Is there a difference between breaking a promise because you can't keep it and breaking a promise because you don't try to keep it?

Can you understand why someone might not keep a promise?

A prayer

Help me to do what I say I will and help me to understand when someone can't keep a promise. Amen.

It Looked That Far to Me
1 John 2:20-21

The Coaker family was eating dinner. Jeff was very excited because his ball team had won an important game.

"We really creamed them," said Jeff. "I just hit that ball every time the pitcher threw it."

"What was the score?" asked Jeff's little brother Andy.

"We beat 'em 8 to 7," said Jeff. "Every time one of them hit a ball to the outfield, I caught it."

"If you only won by one run, it sounds like they have a good team too," said Jeff's father.

"They were just lucky a couple of times," said Jeff. "The first time I was up to bat I hit that ball so far I thought they'd never find it."

"Was it a home run?" asked Andy.

"They got lucky and threw me out at first that time," Jeff said.

"You must not have hit the ball too far if they caught you on first," said Jeff's mother.

"It looked that far to me," said Jeff.

"How many runs did you make?" asked Andy.

"Well, I didn't make any today," said Jeff. "But I did a good job in the outfield."

"I'm sure you enjoyed the game," said his father. "But don't you think you are exaggerating when you say how great you and your team did?"

"No," said Jeff. "You can ask the coach. He said we were all great."

"Your team did play well," said his father. "You won the game. But the other players on your team also played well. And it sounds to me as though the other team played a good game too."

"I guess they did," said Jeff.

"We like to hear how well you play," said Jeff's mother. "But if you exaggerate how well you did, you take away the fun of the real game."

"Jeff always tells lies," said Andy.

"I do not," said Jeff. "I'm a good ball player."

"Sure you are," said his father. "But even good ball players strike out and drop fly balls. They don't have to pretend they never make a mistake."

"Son, we like it when you do well at sports," said his mother. "But we love you just as much when you make an out as when you make a home run. If you stretch the truth, then we can't enjoy the good things that you really did."

"OK," said Jeff. "But I did get on second once. And I'd have made a run except Charlie struck out."

Is stretching the truth the same as lying?

Why do we often exaggerate the truth?

If people brag about things that are not true, will you believe them when they tell the truth?

A prayer

Lord God, help me tell the truth and help me look for the truth from others. In Jesus' name. Amen.

She Picked Me!

Romans 12:6-8

"Hey, Mom! Hey, Mom!" yelled Randy as he ran into the house after school. "She picked me! She picked me!"

"Slow down!" said his mother as the eager boy rushed into her arms. "What happened to you?"

"The teacher picked me," said Randy. "I get to go to a special day at the TV station. Only one from each class gets to go, and Mrs. Hahn picked me."

"That sounds like fun," said his mother. "But I'm still not sure what you're going to do."

"They're having a special day at the TV station," said Randy. "It's to help kids understand how television works. But they can't invite all the kids, so one person from each class in the whole district gets to go."

"That will be interesting," said his mother. "I'm glad Mrs. Hahn picked you."

"Then after I go to the station, I have to come back and tell the rest of the class what happened. That way everyone will know how a TV station works."

"That's great, Randy!" said his mother. "Do you know why Mrs. Hahn picked you?"

"No, I don't," said Randy. "But I'm the only one from my class that gets to go."

"I know that must make you feel good," said his mother. "How do you think the others in your class feel about Mrs. Hahn picking you?"

"They all wanted to go," said Randy. "So I guess they are disappointed."

"I'm sure they are," said his mother. "You will have to do a very good job. If you listen carefully you will be able to tell the rest of the class exactly what happens at the station. Then they will be glad that Mrs. Hahn picked you."

"I'll try hard," said Randy. "I think I can do a good job."

"I think you can too!" said his mother.

Some questions

Are you glad when you are picked to be a leader in your family, class, or other group?

Can you also be glad if someone else is picked to be a leader?

How can you help others be glad that you were picked to be a leader?

A prayer

Dear God, thank you for picking others to help me. Please give me a chance to help others. In Jesus' name. Amen.

She Didn't Pick Me
Luke 22:24-26

"What's the matter with you?" Eric's mother asked as he came home after school.

"Oh, nothing," said Eric.

"You look awfully sad," said his mother.

"She didn't pick me," Eric said.

"Who didn't pick you?" asked his mother.

"Mrs. Hahn didn't pick me to go to the TV station," said Eric. "She picked Randy instead."

"What will Randy get to do?" asked Eric's mother.

"They're having a special day at the TV station so that kids can learn how television works. But they don't have room for everyone, so only one kid from each class gets to go. I wanted to go because I'd like to know about TV. But she didn't pick me."

"I'm sure Randy is glad that he was picked to go," said his mother.

"Yeah," said Eric. "I don't know why she chose him instead of me. I get just as good grades as he does."

"I'm sure Mrs. Hahn had a hard time picking only one student out of the class," said his mother. "That doesn't mean that she likes Randy more. It only means that she had to pick one person."

"She could have picked me," said Eric. "I wanted to see what happens in a TV studio."

"But you will still find out what happens," said his mother. "Randy was picked to represent the class, so he will come back and tell the others what happened. You can ask him questions and talk to him. Then you'll know about TV stations too."

"But I'd rather go myself," said Eric.

"And I'd love for you to go, too," said his mother. "But none of us get to do all the things we want to do. I've learned something important for myself. If I am disappointed about something, I try to do something else to make myself feel good again. Why don't you talk to Randy and do all you can to help him do a good job? That way you will learn about TV too."

"But that won't be as much fun," said Eric.

"Maybe not," said his mother. "But if you learn how to make the best of the situation, you will learn something even more important than how TV works. You will learn to be disappointed without becoming sad or angry."

"Do you think Randy would ask the station manager some questions for me?" asked Eric.

"I'm sure he would," said his mother.

Some questions

If you are willing to be a leader, should you also be willing to be a follower?

Can a disappointment about one thing ruin other things?

Can you help someone else when they are disappointed? Do you let others help you when you are disappointed?

A prayer

Lord Jesus, help me to know when I should lead and when I should follow. Amen.

Enough Money to Buy an Elephant
Matthew 6:19-21

"You know what I'd like to have?" Peter asked his grandfather.

"I can't even guess what you'd like to have," his grandfather answered.

"I'd like to have enough money to buy an elephant," said Peter.

"Why do you want an elephant?" his grandfather asked.

"I didn't say I *want* an elephant," said Peter. "I'd just like enough money to buy one. That would be a lot of money because elephants are very big."

"What would you do with that much money?" asked his grandfather.

"I'd buy you a new fishing rod, I'd buy Mom and Dad a new TV set, I'd put a lot of money in the offering plate at Sunday school, and I'd eat a lot of ice cream," said Peter.

"For the cost of an elephant, I bet you could do all that and still have money left over!" his grandfather said.

"If I had any left over, I'd even buy something for Tina," said Peter. Tina was his older sister.

"It's fun to talk about what you'd do if you had lots of money," said his grandfather. "But it's more important to know what you do with the money you do have. How do you spend your money, Peter?"

"I buy ice cream. And I play games. I've got a surprise for you, but I'm not going to show you until your birthday. And I give some at Sunday school."

"Sounds to me like you must have almost enough money to buy an elephant," said his grandfather.

"I don't have very much money," said Peter.

"But you're doing all the things you said you'd do if you had lots of money," his grandfather said. "I know you gave your mom and dad a nice picture for their wedding anniversary. They like that picture from you as much as they'd like a new TV. I'll enjoy that present from you, no matter what it is."

"But it would be more fun to spend more," said Peter.

"It's not how much you spend," said his grandfather. "It's the love that goes with it that really counts. You give us lots of love."

"Even more love than I could give with an elephant?" asked Peter.

"Lots more!" said his grandfather.

Some questions

What would you do if you had more money?

Do you know other children who have less money than you do?

Does having more money make a person more important than those who have less?

A prayer

Father in heaven, thank you for the money I have. Help me to use it in a good way. In Jesus' name. Amen.

I Want a Baby Sister

Ephesians 3:14-20

"Your birthday is next week, Jessica," said her mother. "Have you thought about anything special that you want as a gift?"

"Yes," said Jessica, "I want a baby sister."

"I'm sure you will not receive a baby sister for your birthday," said her mother. "What else would you like?"

"That's all!" said Jessica. "Just a baby sister."

"Let me explain why you will not get a baby sister," her mother said. "In the first place, it takes a long time to have a baby. Even if we were expecting a baby, you would not have a sister for your birthday. It takes at least nine months to have a baby."

"I can wait," said Jessica.

"Even if we were expecting a baby, we wouldn't know whether it would be a girl or a boy," said her mother.

"A little brother would be all right if that's what we got," said Jessica. "But I already have a brother."

"And your brother already has a sister," said her mother. "And there's another reason why you may not get a baby sister. We already have two children. We love you both very much, but we are not sure that we will have more children."

"There are five kids in Jean's family," said Jessica.

"I know, and we are happy that their family has five children," said her mother. "Uncle Jim and Aunt Marge don't have any children. And the doctor says they will probably never have children."

"I wish they could have a baby," said Jessica. "If we had another one, we could share her with them."

"That's a good idea, but it probably wouldn't work," said her mother. "Each baby is a special gift from God to that baby's parents. You and your brother are God's special gifts to your daddy and me."

"Why doesn't God give each family the same number of babies?" asked Jessica.

"Because each family is different," her mother said. Uncle

149

Jim and Aunt Marge are a family with no children, but they are happy. Jean's family has many children, and they are happy too. We will also be happy with the children we have."

"You can give me something else for my birthday," said Jessica. "But can I still ask God for a baby sister?"

"Yes, you can pray for a baby," said her mother. "But God answers prayers in many different ways. You may not get exactly what you expect."

Some questions

Do you know some families that want to have children but do not have any?

What does it mean to be a family?

Can families who do not have children still be happy and enjoy children from other families?

A prayer

Thank you, God, for making us a family. Help each of us to enjoy the family we have and to share with other families. In Jesus' name. Amen.

I Can't Do That
Philippians 3:12-14

Erin sat very quietly in school and hoped that Mr. Balzer would not notice her. All the other students in the class were busy making a card to send to their mothers on Mother's Day. But Erin was not making a card.

"Are you still deciding what kind of card you want to make?" asked Mr. Balzer as he came to Erin's desk.

"I don't want to make a card," she said.

150

"Mother's Day is next Sunday," said Mr. Balzer, "and I know your mother would like a card that you made."

"Daddy will buy a card for her," said Erin.

"That will be nice," said her teacher. "But I think she would also like a card from you."

"But I can't draw good pictures," said Erin as she watched Sarah draw a beautiful picture of flowers and birds.

"A good picture is one that shows how you feel," said Mr. Balzer. "Your mother would like a picture that you drew for her."

"I'm not neat," said Erin. "What I do always looks messy."

"The card you make is to tell your mother that you love her," said Mr. Balzer. "The card is not meant to tell her that you are neat."

"I'm afraid I can't do it right," said Erin.

"Erin, may I tell you something that I think is important?" asked her teacher. Without waiting for an answer, he added, "You are a good student. I'm glad you are in my class. But I often notice that you are afraid to try to do something new. Can you tell me why you don't like to do new things?"

"I don't know," said Erin. "Maybe because I don't know if I can do it right."

"You'll never find out if you don't try," said Mr. Balzer. "If you draw a picture that you don't like, you can throw it away and start another. You don't have to draw the best picture in the class. If you give your mother something you made, it will be right for her."

Erin looked at the piece of blank paper and the crayons. Then she said, "Will you help me if I don't do it right?"

"I'll help you find out that you can make a pretty card for your mother," said Mr. Balzer. "And I want to help you find out that you can do a lot of other things. You don't have to be perfect in everything you do. Just do the best you can and enjoy it."

"OK," said Erin as she started to draw. "But how will Mom know that this is supposed to be a cat? It doesn't look like a cat to me."

"Easy!" said Mr. Balzer. "Write 'cat' on it."

Do you think it is all right to try to do something and fail?

If you are always afraid that you might do something wrong, is it possible to do anything right?

What things can you do well?

A prayer

Thank you, Jesus, for helping me do some things well and for helping other people do other things well. Amen.

Let's Make This a Happy House
John 15:9-12

The Stewart family was eating dinner. It had not been a good day for the family. Ricky's baseball team had lost a game. Tina had had an argument with her best friend. Mr. Stewart had missed an important appointment at work. Mrs. Stewart had a flat tire on the car. No one was very happy.

"I wish we had a happy house," said Tina about halfway through dinner.

"I thought we did have a happy house," answered her mother.

"Sometimes we do," said Tina, "but it doesn't seem happy now."

"I know why it's not happy tonight," said her father.

"Because everyone is mad and grouchy," said Ricky.

"That's part of the reason," said Mr. Stewart. "But the real reason is that no one brought any happiness into our house tonight. A house can't be happy unless someone brings in the happiness."

"That's right," said Mrs. Stewart. "When someone tracks mud into the house, it is a muddy house. If someone brought happiness in, it would be a happy house."

"I didn't have any happiness to bring because I'm mad at Laura," said Tina.

"And I feel bad because we lost," said Ricky, "so I didn't bring any happiness either."

"I guess I brought problems home from work," said their father, "so I didn't have any happiness to bring home."

"That flat tire ruined my whole day," said Mrs. Stewart. "I was totally out of happiness."

"Let's take turns bringing happiness home," said Tina. "Tomorrow will be my day. I'll bring some happiness home so that we will have a happy house."

"The next day can be my turn," said her father. "We'd better get a calendar so we that can mark down who is to bring the happiness for each day."

"OK," said Ricky, "I'll take the next day—Saturday. That should be an easy day to find something to be happy about."

"Then Sunday is my day," said his mother. "I feel better already. I think we've all helped bring some happiness into our house today."

Some questions

Is your house a happy place?
What kind of feelings do you bring into your house?
Who helps your home to be a happy place?

A prayer

Lord Jesus, please be with us in our family so that we can have a happy house. Amen.

Is God Angry at Me?
2 Corinthians 12:7-8

"Is God angry at me?" Sabrina asked her mother.

"Why, no!" answered her mother. "Why do you ask that?"

"I've been sick for three days," said Sabrina. "My stomach hurts. I can't go to school. God must be mad at me."

"Why would God be mad at you?" asked her mother.

"I don't know," said Sabrina. "Maybe I did something wrong. I told the teacher a lie when I said I lost my homework."

"I'm sorry you told the lie," said her mother. "But God does not make you sick because you told a lie. He sent Jesus to be your Savior. Jesus died to take away all your sins."

"Then why am I sick?" asked Sabrina.

"I don't know why you are sick," her mother said. "But I know that if God made everyone sick when they did something wrong, then everybody would be sick."

"Karen's mother said that if you really love Jesus and pray hard, he will give you everything you ask," said Sabrina. "I asked Jesus to make me well, but I'm still sick."

"What Karen's mother said is not true," said her mother. "God gives us everything we need, but not always what we want. And people who love Jesus still get sick. But they know that Jesus is with them and loves them even when they are sick."

"Will I get well sometime?" asked Sabrina.

"Yes, I believe you will," said her mother. "We will pray every day that God will be with you and heal you. And we will do everything the doctor tells us to do."

"Will the doctor make me well or will Jesus make me well?"

"Jesus will help the doctor make you well," answered her mother. "We have asked God to help. He can help in many ways. One way is through the doctor."

"Then you don't think God is mad at me?" asked Sabrina.

"No," said her mother. "I know God loves you and I know he will always be with you and take care of you."

"I'm glad!" said Sabrina.

Some questions

Do you know that God loves you even when you are sick or have other problems?

When you see someone else who is sick, do you think that person has done something wrong and that God is punishing him or her for it?

How can you help someone who is sick?

A prayer

Dear Jesus, thank you for helping me when I am sick. Please be with (*name some people you know who are sick*) and make them well. Amen.

But It's My Dog
Genesis 1:20-25

Benji and Ernie were playing with a ball in Ernie's backyard.

"Ernie," his mother called, "Romper has been in the garage all day. Take him outside with you."

"Oh, Mom," said Ernie. "Let him stay in there. He's a pain."

"No," said his mother. "He's your dog. You wanted him. Now you take care of him."

Ernie went to the garage to untie Romper. Romper was glad to be free. He ran out into the yard. When Ernie threw the ball to Benji, Romper caught the ball in his mouth and started running.

"Hey, you!" yelled Ernie. "Come back here!" Ernie chased Romper across the yard. When the dog stopped, Ernie kicked him. Romper lay down but held on to the ball. Ernie hit the dog on the head as he grabbed the ball.

"You shouldn't kick your dog," said Benji.

"Why not?" said Ernie. "He's my dog!" He went over to Romper and kicked him again. The dog huddled close to the ground and whined.

"He may be your dog," said Benji, "but that doesn't mean you can hurt him." Benji sat down beside Romper and petted him.

"Don't baby that dog," said Ernie. "He doesn't deserve it."

"He doesn't deserve to be kicked, either," said Benji.

155

"Why not?" asked Ernie. "He always gets in the way. I have to feed him all the time and clean up the mess he makes."

"If you don't want to feed him and clean up his mess, then you shouldn't have a dog," said Benji. "My dad got me a dog so I could learn to be responsible for taking care of it. I don't think you know how to take care of a dog."

"But he's my dog!" said Ernie. "I can do what I want with him."

"No, you can't," said Benji. "My dad says it's against the law to hurt animals. You should either take good care of Romper or give him to someone else."

"Let's stop talking about that dog," Ernie said. "You came over to play; let's play!"

"Only if Romper can play too," said Benji.

"OK," said Ernie, "throw the ball to him."

Some questions

If you have a pet, do you take good care of it?

How do you treat other animals?

What should you do if you see someone hurting an animal?

A prayer

Thank you, God, for creating animals. Help me and others treat them the right way. In Jesus' name. Amen.

You Had a Choice

Luke 9:57-62

Mark and his father had been to a carnival. They had had lots of fun together.

"Here's some money," Mark's father said as they were ready to leave. "Go and buy something from the souvenir stand that will help you remember the fun we had today."

Mark took the money and ran to look at all the souvenirs. First he checked the prices to see which ones he could afford.

"I want either this flag or a balloon. Which do you think I should take?" he asked his father.

"You pick whichever one you want," said his father.

"I'll take the balloon," said Mark, and he paid the person who ran the souvenir stand.

Mark held the balloon in one hand and his father's hand with the other as they walked back to their car. He was very happy. But as he got into the car he pulled the door shut on the balloon. He heard a big bang—and the balloon was gone. All he had was a string and a few little pieces of rubber.

"My balloon broke!" Mark said. "Can I go back and buy the flag?"

"No," said his father. "You had a choice, and you chose the balloon. Balloons are fun, but they don't last long."

"But now I'd rather have the flag," said Mark. "I want something for my room."

"Let's talk about what happened," his father said. "I didn't pick out a gift for you. I wanted you to learn how to make a choice. I want you to know how to make a decision and stick with it."

"But I picked the wrong thing," said Mark.

"No you didn't!" said his father. "A balloon is more fun to play with than a flag. But a flag lasts longer. You were able to choose which one you wanted."

"But now I don't have anything," Mark said, "because the balloon broke."

"But if you had picked the flag, you might have torn it or lost it," his father said. "Don't feel bad! You had the balloon for a while. You also learned something about making a choice. You'll have to make a lot of choices in your life. I think you'll learn how to make good choices."

"OK," said Mark. "Now I choose that we go home fast. I'm hungry!"

Some questions

What decisions do you get to make for yourself?
Whom can you ask to help you make a decision?
Do you think anyone always makes the right choice?

Dear God, thank you for letting me have many choices in my life. Help me choose the right things. In Jesus' name. Amen.

Look What You Gave Me
Psalm 127:3-5

"Come here, Rachel!" her father called. "I want to show you something I just found."

Rachel ran to the living room where her father was reading a book. "What did you find?" she asked.

"I found something you gave me a long time ago," answered her father. "Look at this!"

"What is it?" asked Rachel as she looked at the piece of red paper in her father's hand.

"It's an outline of your hand when you were three years old," said her father. "You put your hand on the paper and traced around it. Then you gave me the picture for Father's Day."

"Let me see," said Rachel. She put her hand on the picture. "My hand is a lot bigger now."

"Yes, you've grown a lot. And you'll grow a lot more."

"Where did you find this?" asked Rachel.

"It was in this book," said her father. "When you gave it to me I put it in there as a bookmark. When I opened the book today I found it."

"Why did you keep it?" asked Rachel.

"Because I was happy when you gave me the picture," her father said. "I wanted to keep it to remember that day."

"I didn't draw very well," said Rachel. "My fingers look funny."

"You were three years old," said her father. "You did a good job and you made me happy. When I look at this, I remember how much I enjoyed being your daddy."

"Are you still glad you are my daddy?" she asked.

"Of course!" he said. "You are still my precious little gift from God—only you aren't so little anymore."

What have you done that made other members of your family happy?

What have other members of your family done that made you happy?

A prayer

Thank you, God, for everyone in my family. Help me enjoy them and help them enjoy me. In Jesus' name. Amen.

I Can't Find My Teddy
Luke 18:15-17

Kevin wanted to cry, but he didn't think he should. He knew it was all right for boys to cry. He saw his dad cry once when his mother was sick. But this was different: he couldn't find his Teddy.

When he was very little, Kevin had a special teddy bear. He always called it his Teddy. He carried it with him everywhere he went and it got dirty and tattered, but he still liked it. As he grew older he did not carry his Teddy around anymore, but he kept it in a box in his cupboard. When he had the measles, he took his Teddy out of the box for a while.

When Kevin's family moved to a new house, he was busy with many things and forgot about his Teddy. One day he remembered the old toy and went to look for it. When he couldn't find it anywhere, he asked his mother where it was.

"I don't know what happened to it," said his mother. "When we moved, we packed everything that was in your room. I'll help you look for it."

Kevin and his mother looked everywhere, but they didn't find the stuffed toy.

"I'm sorry we can't find your Teddy," said his mother. "I know it was important to you."

"That's OK," said Kevin, even though he didn't feel it was OK. "Teddy bears are for little kids."

"But when you grow older, you don't have to forget the things that were important to you when you were little," said his mother. "When I was a little girl, I had a doll that I loved very much. I don't have the doll anymore, but I still remember how I used to sit in a playhouse with it."

"So do you still enjoy that doll?" asked Kevin.

"Yes, it is a good memory," said his mother. "You can have good memories about your Teddy, too. Remembering the things you did when you were a little boy is an important part of your life."

"And now I am growing up," said Kevin.

"Yes, you are," said his mother. "As you grow up, you are adding to your life. But you don't have to give up what you were when you were little."

Some questions

Do you remember toys that were important to you when you were very little?

What do you like now that will be an important part of your memories when you grow up?

A prayer

Dear Jesus, help me to learn how to be happy now, and how to make other people happy too. Amen.

But I Wanted a Baseball Glove
Philippians 4:10-13

Todd was excited when a package arrived from his grandparents one week before Christmas. When he'd talked to his grandmother on the phone, he had told her he was going to play baseball next year. He had mentioned that he would need a new baseball glove if he was going to play with a real team.

The box that came from his grandparents had a package with his name on it. Every day Todd would feel the package under the Christmas tree. It wasn't exactly the right shape for a baseball glove, but it felt the right weight. He couldn't hear anything when he shook it. But he knew it had to be a glove.

On Christmas Day, Todd was excited as he opened all his gifts one by one. At last he came to the package from his grandparents. It was a pair of shoes.

"But I wanted a baseball glove," he said. "I told Grandma I was going to play with a real team this year."

"Todd, remember that these shoes are a gift to you," said his mother. "Your grandparents thought about you. They even got the right size. It is a nice gift."

"But I wanted a baseball glove," he said.

"You'll still be able to have a new glove," said his mother. "You already have some money. You can save more from your allowance. I'm sure we can find some jobs for you to do if you need to earn some extra money to buy the glove."

"But Grandma and Grandpa could have given me the glove," said Todd.

"They gave you a nice gift," said his mother. "Don't let your need for a glove keep you from enjoying what you received. A gift is something people want to give. Your grandparents wanted to give you the shoes. Maybe they thought it would be better for you to earn the glove for yourself."

"I guess you're right," said Todd. "Now I can pick out exactly the kind of glove I want."

Some questions

Do you know how to accept a gift?

Would you rather have a gift that you need or one that you want?

Do you like to give gifts to others?

A prayer

Dear God, thank you for the gifts you have given to me and also for the gifts that others have given me. In Jesus' name. Amen.

Happy Memories
John 14:25-27

Stacy liked to visit her great-grandmother who lived in a nursing home. Her great-grandmother told her stories from a long time ago. Stacy especially liked to hear about the times when her great-grandmother lived on a farm and walked to a country school. She liked to hear about the farm animals, the snow, the wildflowers, and the farm buildings.

"Do you have pictures of the farm and school?" Stacy once asked the old woman.

"I used to have pictures," her great-grandmother said. "We lost a lot of them in a fire when your grandfather was a little boy. Then when I moved from place to place I always had to leave some things behind. They're all gone now."

"Do you have toys that you played with when you were a little girl?" asked Stacy.

"No, not anymore," said her great-grandmother. "I had some toys and I enjoyed them. But they're long gone."

"Do you have lots of money from selling the farm?" asked Stacy.

"No, times were bad in those days—very bad. So we didn't get much money for the farm," answered her great-grandmother. "But I have something more important than money, or pictures, or things in boxes and books."

"What do you have?" asked Stacy.

"I have happy memories," said the old woman. "When I was a little girl, I didn't think I'd grow up to be rich or famous. But my mother told me I could have happy memories. And those are more important. I didn't have to leave them behind each time I moved."

"Can I have happy memories too?" asked Stacy.

"Sure you can, sweetheart!" said her great-grandmother. "Look at things that are pretty—the flowers, the sky, the water. Be with people who laugh and talk."

"Will that give me happy memories when I am old?" asked Stacy.

163

"Yes, it will!" her great-grandmother said. "I like to remember how God has made me happy in the past. And I know he'll make me happy from now on too. If you've got happy memories of the past, you've also got happy hopes for the future."

Some questions

What have you done lately that will give you happy memories in the future?

Do you know people who can show you how to be happy?

A prayer

Dear God, take away unhappy things and give me your joy, so that I may have a happy life now and forever. In Jesus' name. Amen.

Three Little Books That Went to School
Matthew 25:14-27

On the first day of school, Miss Hahn was ready to give her third-grade class their books.

"Before I give you your books for this year, I want to tell you a story," said the teacher. "The name of the story is 'Three Little Books That Went to School.' "

"The first little book that went to school was in the third grade. It was given to a student who never used it. He never opened it to read it. He never took it with him to do his homework. He kept it in the back of his desk. At the end of the year the first little book looked like this." Miss Hahn held up a new book with no marks on it.

"Do you think the first little book that went to school was happy?" she asked. "No, the first little book was not happy. It had something to teach the student to whom it was given. But no one studied the first little book."

"The second little book was given to a student who studied it. But he also drew pictures all over the book. He threw the book at other students. He tore pages from the book to make paper wads that he threw at other students. At the end of the year the second little book that went to school looked like this." The teacher showed the class a badly damaged book.

"Do you think this book was happy?" asked Miss Hahn. "No, it was not happy. It only lasted one year. Then it had to be thrown away."

"The third little book was given to a student who did his lessons well. He read the book every day. He took it home to study. He put his name in it. He underlined some important parts of the book and he marked the assignments that the teacher gave him. But he made all the marks with a pencil so that they could be erased when he finished the third grade. At the end of the year the third little book that went to school looked like this." The teacher showed a used book that was neat and ready to be used again.

"Do you think this book was happy?" asked Miss Hahn. "Yes, it was happy because it had been used. But it wasn't misused; so it could be given to another student the next year."

"Now I will give you your books. I hope you will use them the right way so that both you and your book will be glad you are in the third grade this year."

Some questions

Do you know how to take care of property?

Do you take good care of things that you own?

Do you take good care of things that you use but do not own (parks, your school, church, library, etc.)?

A prayer

Father in heaven, thank you for making many wonderful things for us to use. Help us take good care of them. In Jesus' name. Amen.

The Teacher Doesn't Like Me

Luke 6:37-38

"Mrs. Mann moved away," Ann told her mother when she came home from school. "We've got a new teacher, and she doesn't like me."

"What makes you think she doesn't like you?" her mother asked.

"Because she won't let me be Snow White in the school play," said Ann as tears streamed down her face. "Mrs. Mann had picked me for the part; I already knew one of the songs. Now the new teacher says Laura is to be Snow White and I have to be in the chorus."

"Maybe the new teacher didn't know that Mrs. Mann had already picked you for the part," said her mother.

"Oh, Mom, you always think the teacher is right!" said Ann. "She knew I was supposed to be Snow White. Mrs. Mann left a paper with all the names on it. The new teacher changed everything."

"Do you want me to talk to the new teacher?" asked her mother.

"No, because Laura's my friend," Ann said. "She thinks she is going to be Snow White now. I told her I didn't mind, because I know it's not her fault. But I don't think it's fair."

"I agree that it's not fair," said Ann's mother. "But I'm afraid that some things in life are not fair."

"Why doesn't she like me?" asked Ann. "She didn't even give me a chance to sing by myself. She listened to all of us singing together, and then she picked the kids to be Snow White, the Prince, and others who get to sing by themselves."

"Each teacher has to do things her own way," said her mother. "When Mrs. Mann picked you, Laura probably thought she could do it as well as you could—but Mrs. Mann picked you. Now the new teacher picked Laura. It doesn't mean the new teacher doesn't like you. Mrs. Mann liked Laura, but she picked you for the part."

"I know," said Ann. "But it's still not fair. I'm glad we've only got two more months of school. I can look forward to a new teacher next year."

Some questions

Do you think other people can always be fair to you?
Do you think you are always fair to other people?

A prayer

Dear Jesus, help me to be fair to others and help me not cause problems when others are unfair to me. Amen.

Words Can Hurt
Matthew 5:21-22

Jill was helping set the table for dinner. When she moved a bowl to make room for a platter, she knocked a plate off the table. Jill started to cry as she looked down at the broken plate.

"Hey, dummy!" yelled Bobby. "How come you're so clumsy? You broke a plate."

"Don't worry, Jill," said her mother as she brought a broom. "It was an accident. Help me pick up all the pieces so that no one will be hurt by stepping on them."

"I'm sorry I broke the plate," sobbed Jill.

"I know it was an accident," said her mother. "Don't get upset."

"But Bobby called me a dummy," said Jill. "I didn't mean to do anything wrong."

"Well, she *is* a dummy," said Bobby. "She drops things all the time."

"No, she is not a dummy," said her mother. "She is five years old and she is learning to help. You should not call her bad names. Words can hurt."

"You called me a dummy when I tripped over the vacuum cleaner," said Bobby.

"I'm sorry that I said that," said his mother. "I was wrong. You are not a dummy. You do things very well."

"Then why did you yell at me for saying the same thing you say?" asked Bobby.

"I didn't realize I had called you that," said his mother. "When I was a little girl, my father always said I was clumsy. It made me feel so bad that I worried about it. That made me all the more clumsy. I'm afraid I did the same thing to you."

"You don't think I'm clumsy?" asked Bobby.

"Of course not!" said his mother. "Anyone can trip over things left on the floor. I said something without thinking."

"Then I guess Jill isn't a dummy either," said Bobby. "But that was my plate she broke. Where do I find another one?"

Some questions

Have you been hurt when someone called you bad names?

Do you think you may have hurt others by calling them bad names?

What words hurt you?

A prayer

Lord Jesus, forgive me for having called other people bad names, and help me forgive those who have called me bad names. Amen.

I'm Not Talking
Matthew 18:15-17

The Moore family was eating dinner. Ted was eagerly telling everyone about his art project at school. The parents were talking about buying new tires for the car. But Vickie was eating without saying a word.

"Vickie, you haven't said anything all evening," said Mrs. Moore. "Do you feel all right?"

"I'm not talking," said Vickie.

"She's mad about something," said Ted, "so she's pouting."

"What is the matter?" asked her mother.

Vickie didn't say a word.

"She always does that," said Ted. "She always pouts if she doesn't get her way."

"Ted, keep quiet for a little bit!" said his father. "Vickie, if there's something wrong you should tell us. We love you and want to help you, but we can't help you if we don't know what's wrong."

Vickie still didn't say anything.

"When you pout, you are making the rest of us guess what is wrong," said her mother. "That's not fair. We have a movie to watch on the VCR tonight; it's for the whole family. If you can't talk to us as a family, you can't be with us to watch the movie."

"That's not fair!" said Vickie. "You're not fair to me. You love Ted but you don't love me."

"Why do you feel that way?" asked her mother. "We love both of you."

"You gave Ted a candy bar in his lunch at school," said Vickie, "but you didn't give me one."

"I didn't put a candy bar in Ted's lunch," said his mother.

"Yes, you did!" said Vickie. "I was in the lunchroom at the same time his class was, and I saw him eating it."

"The teacher gave me that candy bar," said Ted. "It was the prize I won for my art project."

Vickie looked surprised.

"It's important for you to talk about things that worry you, Vickie," said her mother. "You were angry about something that didn't happen. Do you feel better now?"

"Yes," said Vickie.

"Good!" said her father. "Let's get the dishes done quickly so that we can watch the movie."

Some questions

Do you know people who pout?

Do other people think you pout?

How can we help people who pout?

A prayer

Dear God, help me talk to others when I am angry with them and help me listen to those who are angry with me. In Jesus' name. Amen.

When I Was Your Age
Luke 2:25-33

"Hey, Randy," his father called, "look at what I found!"

"What is it?" asked Randy as he ran into his parents' bedroom.

"Here is a picture of me when I was your age," said his father.

"Let me see it," said Randy. He took the picture and saw a small boy standing by a bicycle.

"That was my first bike," said his father. "See, it still had training wheels on it."

"I can ride a bike without training wheels already," said Randy. "What happened to the bike?"

"I'm not sure," said his father. "I had it for a long time. I guess it finally wore out."

"Do I look like you did?" asked Randy.

"Your grandmother thinks so," said his father. "What do you think?"

"You needed a haircut," said Randy.

"That's the way kids wore their hair then," said his father. "See, I had freckles, just like you do."

"But you don't have freckles now," said Randy.

"Freckles generally go away when you grow up," his father said.

"Will mine go away?" asked Randy.

"I suppose so," said his father. "I know you don't like your freckles, but I do. They make you look like a nice little boy."

"I hope they go away when I get bigger," said Randy. "How tall were you then?"

"Let's see," said his father. "Seeing myself beside that bike reminds me that I was always a short kid. I had a hard time reaching the pedals."

"But you're tall now," said Randy, who always felt so little beside his daddy.

"I'm sure you are bigger now than I was at that age," said his father. "I didn't start growing until I was in high school. Do you want to keep this picture?"

"Sure!" said Randy. "I'll put it beside my school picture. We'll look like brothers."

Some questions

Would you like to know more about your parents when they were your age? What would you like to know more about?

Do you think your parents may have worried about some of the same things that you worry about?

A prayer

Father in heaven, help me to enjoy being a child, and help me to grow up to be a happy teenager. In Jesus' name. Amen.

Take Your Medicine
Mark 8:22-25

When Kara had been sick for two days, her mother took her to the doctor. He said she should not go back to school for several days. Then he wrote a prescription for some medicine. On the way home, Kara's mother had the prescription filled.

"The doctor said to start taking the medicine right away," her mother said when they got home.

"I don't want to take pills," said Kara.

"Daddy and I don't take pills unless it's absolutely necessary," said her mother. "And we don't want you to take them either, unless a doctor says you should. This time the doctor said you should."

"Will they taste like sweets?" asked Kara.

"No," said her mother. "This is medicine."

"Will they taste bad?" asked Kara.

"No, I don't think they have any taste," said her mother. "They are not like food."

"Why do I have to take them?" asked Kara.

"Because you are sick," her mother said. "You have an infection in your body that is hurting you. These pills will help your body get rid of the infection."

"Can't we pray and ask God to make me well?" asked Kara.

"Yes," said her mother. "We have been praying for you each day, and we will keep on praying for you. God is answering our prayers by giving us a good doctor and providing this medicine for you."

"If I take the medicine, will I be able to go back to school next week?" asked Kara.

"I think so," said her mother. "The doctor said you are doing fine. Now let's stop talking and start swallowing!"

Some questions

Who are some people who have helped you stay healthy?

What are some things you can do to stay healthy?

What are some things you can do when you are ill?

A prayer

Lord Jesus, thank you for healing many people. Help me and others to stay well, and bless us when we are ill. Amen.

What Can I Do?

John 13:31-35

"Rick, I'm going over to visit Mrs. Miller in a little while," said his mother. "Would you like to go along?"

"Do I have to?" asked Rick.

"No, you don't have to go," said his mother. "But Mrs. Miller has been sick in bed for a long time. She likes company."

"But what can I do over there?" Rick asked.

"You can help Mrs. Miller," answered his mother.

"How can I help her?" asked Rick. "She can't do anything and I can't make her well again."

"No, you can't make her well," said his mother. "But you can make her feel better."

"Why would she feel better if I went to see her?" Rick asked.

"Because she's alone and she likes company," said his mother. "I'm going to take this magazine along. We can talk with her for a while; then I'll leave her the magazine."

"But what can I talk to her about?" asked Rick.

"Mrs. Miller likes children. She likes to hear about your school and your friends," said his mother. "Maybe you could take a game along. She likes to play games."

"Would she know how to play Ladders and Slides?"

"I think she would," said his mother. "If not, you could teach her how to play. All three of us could play that."

"But I'd rather play with my friends," said Rick.

"I'm glad you enjoy your friends. But I also hope you learn how to enjoy helping other people. I makes me happy to be able to help Mrs. Miller. I'm glad she likes you and always asks about you. That means you have helped her too."

"Do you think she might have some nice things to eat?"

"She usually does," said his mother with a smile.

Some questions

Whom would you like to visit you if you were ill?

Do you know anyone who is ill whom you could visit?

How can you make lonely people happy?

A prayer

Lord Jesus, help me to love other people the way you have loved me. Amen.

But I Tried Hard

James 1:2-8

"Andy," his mother called. "I want to talk to you."

"I'm busy now," he answered. Andy had brought home his report card from school that afternoon. He knew that his mother wanted to talk about it.

"We're going to talk now," said his mother as she came into his room carrying the report card. "We have to discuss this."

"All right," said Andy. "I got a 'B' in writing!"

"Yes, so I see," said his mother. "I'm glad that you can write neatly. But some of these other grades are not as good."

"But I tried hard," said Andy.

"Mr. Hanson doesn't seem to think so," said his mother. "In the effort column, you got an 'unsatisfactory' in both reading and arithmetic. You also got a 'D' in both subjects."

"I'll do better next time," Andy said.

"That's what you told me after your last report card," said his mother. "We've had your eyes checked. I've talked to the school principal. I've offered to help you in every way I can. You must do something to improve."

"The trouble is, Mr. Hanson doesn't like me," said Andy.

"No, you can't blame your teacher," his mother said. "I've talked to him, and he has done everything he can to help you. He tells me you don't hand in your assignments and that you don't pay attention in class."

"I'll do better next time," said Andy.

"I'm going to help you," his mother said. "I will ask Mr. Hanson to send a book home with you every night. You will not watch any TV until you do your homework and do some reading for me."

"Can I still watch the Saturday cartoons?" asked Andy.

"No," said his mother. "We'll get some good books from the library and we'll read together on Saturday morning."

"Can I pick out the books?" asked Andrew.

"Yes," said his mother. "We'll go to the library right after school tomorrow. You can pick two books and I will pick two books."

Some questions

Do you need help in doing your schoolwork? If you do, how can your parents help you?

Do you know other students in your class who need help? Can you do anything to help them?

A prayer

Dear God, help me to learn all the things I need to learn at school and help (*name some of your friends*) learn too. In Jesus' name. Amen.

I Don't Like Broccoli
1 Corinthians 13:11

"I don't want any of that!" said Jennifer as her mother started to put broccoli on her plate at dinner.

"Oh yes you do!" said her mother. "You do want some broccoli. It's good for you."

"But I don't like broccoli!" said Jennifer.

"Are you sure you don't like it?" asked her mother. "I'm not sure you have ever tasted it."

"Yes I have," said Jennifer. "We've had it before and it tastes yukky."

"I eat broccoli," said Jennifer's father. "I think it tastes good."

"But you think everything tastes good," said Jennifer. "I don't like it."

"I like most foods now," said her father, "but when I was little I didn't like spinach or carrots."

"Did you like broccoli?" asked Jennifer.

"I can't remember," said her father. "I don't think we had broccoli in those days. But I like it now. I also like spinach and carrots."

"My family had broccoli when I was little," said her mother. "At first I didn't like it. But my mother got me to eat just a little at a time. Now I think it's delicious."

"I think it's yukky!" said Jennifer.

"You don't have to eat a full helping," said her mother. "But you do need good food at each meal. So instead of dessert I'll give you raisins and an apple."

"But I'd rather have dessert," said Jennifer.

"I know," said her mother, "but you need good food to help you grow. Since I want our mealtimes to be happy, I won't force you to eat the broccoli. The fruit will be good for you."

"If I eat one little piece of broccoli, can I have some dessert?" asked Jennifer.

"Yes," said her mother. "If you eat a little helping, I think you will learn to like broccoli just like I did."

Some questions

What are your favorite foods? Are they all good for you? What foods do you not like? Do you need some of those foods so that you can be healthy and strong?

A prayer

Thank you, God, for all food. Help me eat the foods that are good for me. In Jesus' name. Amen.

I Want to Sit by the Window

Ephesians 5:1-2

"I want to sit by the window," said Tracy as she ran to the car.

"No, it's not your turn," said her brother Rick. "You had the window the last time."

"You two can fight over that window; I've got this one," said their sister Rachel as she ran to the right rear door of the family car and got in.

Tracy and Rick each held on to the handle of the left car door. Neither could get in as they argued about who would sit by the window.

"What's going on here?" asked their father as he came out of the house.

"It's my turn to sit by the window," said Tracy, "and he won't let me in."

"I'll let you in," said Rick. "But whoever gets in first has to sit in the middle."

"Then you go in first," said Tracy. "It's my turn to sit on the outside. I sat in the middle when we went to Grandma's."

"But that's only a 10-minute ride," said Rick. "This time we'll be in the car for over an hour, won't we, Dad?"

"Yes, we have a long ride," said their father. "And we are not going to have the three of you arguing during the whole trip."

"I'm not arguing!" said Rachel smugly.

"That's because you grabbed the other window seat," said Rick. "You have to sit in the middle sometimes too."

"I sat in the middle when we went to church," said Rachel.

"Every time our family goes for a drive I hear this same argument," said their father. "We need a way to solve it."

"I know!" said Rick. "The older kids sit by the window and the little one sits in the middle."

"No," said Tracy, "girls sit by the windows and boys sit in the middle."

"I think I'll have to settle this," their father said. "Do you see the three seat belts? This is number one, this is number two, and this is number three. Today the oldest sits in number one, the next in number two, and the youngest in number three."

"That's not fair," said Rachel, "because I get the middle."

"But on the way home, each one moves over one," said their father. "You will be in number three, your brother in the middle, and Tracy by the other window. Each time we take a trip, we will move over one seat."

"But some trips are longer than others," said Rick.

"That's right," said their father. "No system is fair to everyone all the time. But this is the way we will do it. There will be no arguing."

Some questions

Do you think the father's solution was fair?

How would you have solved the problem?

If there are only one or two children in your family, you may not have had this problem. Is there some other problem to be solved?

A prayer

Dear Jesus, help me be fair to other people, and help them be fair to me. Amen.

I Don't Like What You Said

Ephesians 4:29-32

"The phone is for you, Susie," said her mother. "Don't stay on too long. It's Joni."

"Hi, Joni!" said Susie as she picked up the phone. "What do you want?"

"Hi!" said Joni. "I want to find out why you're mad at me."

"I'm not mad at you," Susie said.

"You walked off and left us at the playground without even saying good-bye," Joni said.

"I just decided to go home," said Susie.

178

"You didn't have to go home that early," said Joni. "And we didn't know why you left without saying anything."

"I didn't like what you were talking about," Susie said.

"What were we talking about?" asked Joni.

"You were saying bad things about Sara," said Susie.

"What were we saying about her?" asked Joni.

"You were laughing at her because she has a birthmark on her face," answered Susie.

"She does have a birthmark on her face," said Joni.

"That doesn't mean you have to make fun of her," Susie said.

"What do you care?" Joni said. "You don't have a birthmark."

"Yes, I do!" said Susie.

"I've never seen it," said Joni.

"And you aren't going to see it!" Susie said. "But just because you can see Sara's birthmark doesn't mean you should say bad things about her."

"We didn't mean to hurt her," said Joni.

"Would you have said those things if Sara was there?" asked Susie.

"No," Joni said.

"Now that you know I have a birthmark, will you tell the others and laugh at me?" Susie asked.

"Of course not!" said Joni.

"OK, then we're still friends," said Susie. "But I've got to go. My mother said I couldn't be on the phone too long."

Some questions

Do you think Susie did the right thing when she walked away from the others who were saying bad things about Sara?

Should Susie have stayed and defended Sara?

What can you do when you hear people saying bad things about others?

A prayer

Dear Jesus, forgive me for the bad things I have said about others, and help me think and say good things. Amen.

Do I Have to Go to Church?

Hebrews 10:23-25

"Time to get ready for church!" called Sarah's father as he came into the room where she was watching cartoons on TV.

"Aw, Dad," said Sarah. "Do I *have* to go?"

"Yes, the whole family is going," said her father.

"Why do I have to go along?" she asked. "You get a baby-sitter for me when you go to a movie. Can I have a baby-sitter now?"

"We don't take you along just because we don't have a baby-sitter," said her father as he sat down beside her. "We want you to come with us to church because church is for you too."

"Why should I go?" asked Sarah.

"Because you are a part of the church," said her father. "Jesus loves you—just as he loves all of us."

"But Jesus would love me even if I didn't go to church, wouldn't he?" asked Sarah.

"Of course he would!" said her father. "And I would also love you even if I didn't see you for a long time."

"But Jesus can see me at home and I can pray to him here," said Sarah.

"Yes, you can," said her father. "But when we go to church we are helping other people in God's family and letting them help us. That's what happens when we hear God's Word and worship him."

"How do people help me in church?" asked Sarah.

"They teach you about Jesus and help you remember the things God does for you," said her father. "They love you and help you know that you are not alone. You are part of a congregation of people who care about one another."

"How do I help them by going to church?" asked Sarah. She liked her father to spend time with her alone. She was sure he would stay with her as long as she kept asking questions.

"You make other people happy when you love them and talk to them," said her father. "Most people love children. They like to see you in church with them. You help older people when you show them that you love Jesus too."

"But what if some people don't see me?" Sarah asked. "I just ran out of answers," said her father, "and you just ran out of time. Now get dressed!"

Some questions

Why do you like (or not like) to go to church?
Do you look forward to seeing anyone at church?
Do you think anyone looks forward to seeing you at church?

A prayer

Lord Jesus, thanks for loving me. Please help me to worship you and to enjoy being with other people who love you. Amen.

Don't Waste Food
John 6:1-13

"Tom!" his mother called. "Come here!"

"What do you want, Mom?" Tom answered.

"Look what I found in the garbage can," said his mother.

"Yeah," said Tom. "Garbage."

"No, this should not be garbage," his mother said. "Here is a sandwich and a banana that I put in your lunch. What are they doing in the garbage?"

"I was full," said Tom, "so I threw the rest of my lunch away."

"You should not have thrown good food away," said his mother. "You should have put it in the refrigerator and eaten it later."

"If I didn't want it now," said Tom, "I wouldn't want it later, either."

"But this is good food," said his mother, "and you shouldn't waste it."

"What difference does it make?" asked Tom. "If I had eaten it it would have been gone. And if I throw it in the garbage it's also gone."

"We paid for the food," said his mother, "and we should not waste it."

"Oh, Mom," said Tom. "We can afford to throw away half a sandwich and a banana."

"Yes, we can afford to," said his mother, "but we are not going to. Just because we have enough money to buy all the food we need does not give us the right to throw it away."

"Why not?" asked Tom. "It's our money."

"The world only produces so much food," said his mother, "and many people are hungry. If we use our money to buy food that we waste, there will be less food for others."

"But they can't afford it anyway," said Tom.

"But when we waste food we make the prices go higher," said his mother.

"OK, OK," said Tom. "I won't waste any more food. Why are you so upset about wasting food?"

"Because I'm about to send some of this week's grocery money to a relief agency to help feed hungry children in other countries," said his mother. "Would you like to send some of your money with mine?"

"Will fifty cents do?" Tom asked.

"How about a dollar?" she suggested.

"OK, you've got it."

Some questions

Do you know people who do not have enough to eat? Do you know about people in other countries who are hungry?

What can you do to help hungry people?

A prayer

Father in heaven, thank you for the food I have to eat. Help me to share what I have with others. In Jesus' name. Amen.

I Can't Stay Overnight
Psalm 4

Megan was eager to get to school. Her mother had told her she could invite her new friend Crystal to stay overnight. She knew they would have lots of fun. As soon as Megan got to school, she looked for her friend.

"Hi, Crystal!" said Megan. "My mother said I could invite you to come home with me after school on Friday. Can you come?"

"I'll have to ask my parents," said Crystal. "Will your father take me home or should my daddy come and get me?"

"I want you to stay all night," said Megan. "Then we'll take you home on Saturday."

"I can't stay with you," said Crystal.

"Why not?" asked Megan. "You haven't even asked your mother yet."

"Maybe I can go home with you after school," said Crystal, "but I can't stay overnight."

"Don't say you can't," said Megan. "Ask your mother."

"I know I can't stay overnight," Crystal said.

"Your mother won't let you?" asked Megan.

"I don't want to," said Crystal.

"You don't want to!" said Megan. "We'll make popcorn and play games. We'll have lots of fun."

"No, I can't," Crystal said.

"Why not?" Megan asked.

"You're my friend," said Crystal. "Can I tell you a big secret?"

"Sure!" answered Megan. "You can tell me anything."

"Sometimes at night I have a problem," said Crystal. "Sometimes I wet the bed."

"You mean you still wet the bed?" asked Megan.

"My mother took me to a doctor," Crystal said. "He says he thinks he can help me. I don't do it every night."

"Then why can't you stay at my house?" Megan asked.

"I don't want to ruin your bed," said Crystal.

"What do you do at home?" asked Megan.

"My mother made a special pad for me," Crystal said.

"Could you bring it along to my house?" Megan asked.

"I guess I could," said Crystal, "if your mother says it's OK."

"I'm sure my mom will agree," said Megan. "Let's phone your mother."

Some questions

Do you (or does someone you know) have problems with bed wetting?

Would you laugh at a person who had such a problem?

Are there other problems that worry you?

A prayer

Dear God, help other people to understand my problems and help me to understand theirs. In Jesus' name. Amen.

Another Commandment
1 John 4:16-19

"What did you study in Sunday school today, Shawn?" his mother asked as they drove home from church.

"We studied the Ten Commandments," said Shawn.

"Do you know all of them?" his mother asked.

"I think so," said Shawn, "but there should be one more."

"Do you think we need another commandment?" asked his mother.

"Yes," Shawn said. "There should be one that says, 'You must love Jesus.' "

"Why do you think we need that commandment?" asked his mother.

"Because that's the most important thing," said Shawn. "I know it's important not to steal or lie and things like that. But it's more important that we love Jesus. He's the one who died for us so that our sins could be forgiven."

"I agree that loving Jesus is very important," said his mother. "In fact, it's so important that we need more than a commandment to help us do it."

"What do you mean?" asked Shawn.

"God gave us 10 commandments, but we keep breaking them," she said. "And God loves us so much that he tried another way to get us to follow his will."

"What did he do?" asked Shawn.

"He sent Jesus to be our Savior," said his mother. "And after Jesus died for us, God brought him back to life again so he could live inside us. Jesus not only takes away our sin, he also lives in us so we can love God."

"He could have just given us a commandment that says we have to love him," said Shawn.

"That wouldn't work," said his mother. "God can't force us to love him, any more than I can make you love me. But when we are forgiven and Jesus lives inside us, we want to love God and each other."

"That's kind of nice, huh?" said Shawn.

"It sure is," said his mother. "Sometimes I just don't feel like doing the things I should do. I don't need another commandment then—I need Jesus."

"OK, so we don't need another commandment," Shawn said. "But how about an ice-cream cone?"

"How about lunch when we get home?" his mother suggested.

Some questions

Are there times when you don't feel like loving God or other people? Would it help to be told that you have to?

Are there times when you *do* feel like loving God and other people? Who or what has helped you feel that way?

A prayer

Lord Jesus, thank you for loving us and helping us all the time. Help us love you. Amen.

Let's Read a Book!

2 Timothy 3:14-17

"Come on, Jeff," said his father, "turn off the TV. Let's read a book!"

"I want to watch this program," said Jeff.

"I'm going to be gone tomorrow night," said his father. "I want to spend time with you now. I'd like to read you a book."

"We can watch TV together," suggested Jeff.

"Then we just sit in the same room," said his father. "If I read to you, we can pick what we want and we can talk to each other."

"OK," said Jeff as he turned off the TV and crawled up on his father's lap. "What are you going to read?"

"What would you like to read?" asked his father.

"Most of the time you read from *God's Love for God's Children*," Jeff said.

"And what else?" asked his father.

"We always read the Bible first," answered Jeff.

"I'm glad we read the Bible and have devotions together," said his father. "When you have grown up, I'm sure you will remember the things we read and talked about."

"Will I remember that we watched TV together?" asked Jeff.

"Maybe," said his father, "but I think reading does more to help us think and talk to each other. When we watch TV, someone else is doing our talking and thinking for us. They show us what to think. When we read books, we have to use our imagination."

"What's an imagination?" asked Jeff.

"It's when you see things in your mind," said his father.

"Instead of seeing them on a TV set?" asked Jeff.

"Yes, sort of," said his father. "You have a good imagination. Remember when I read the book about the spaceship? You pretended you landed on Mars."

187

"It was hot up there," said Jeff. "But I found a Coke machine."
"I told you you had a good imagination!" said his father.
"OK, let's read a book," said Jeff. "You pick one."

Some questions

Who reads to you?
Do you think there is someone else who would read to you
if you asked?
What books do you like to hear read?

A prayer

Thank you, God, for books and for people who can read
them. Help me to learn to read more and more. In Jesus' name.
Amen.

Can I Believe You?
Ephesians 4:15-16

"I need a dollar," Benji told his father.
"Why?" asked his father.
"For paper at school," he answered.
"I gave you a dollar for paper last week," said his father.
"I lost it," Benji said.
"Is that the truth?" his father asked.
"Yes," said Benji.
"You told me you lost your lunch money last week," said his
father, "but your teacher said you bought ice cream instead of
lunch."
"I'm sorry I lied to you," said Benji.
"If you had told me the truth then, I would believe you now,"
said his father. "I saw you eating candy after school yesterday.
Where did you get it?"
"Chuck gave it to me," said Benji.
"I'm sorry, I can't believe you," said his father. "I will check
with Chuck about the candy."

"Fine," said Benji, "but he's gone for the week. He went to visit his grandmother. And I need the dollar now."

"First you and I are going to see Chuck's mother," said his father.

"Why?" Benji asked.

"To ask when Chuck will be home."

"He was gone yesterday," said Benji. "Maybe he came home today."

"You said he gave you the candy yesterday," said his father.

"Maybe Carl gave it to me," said Benji.

"Or maybe you told me a lie," said his father.

"Maybe," Benji said.

"You told me one lie when you said you needed paper," his father said. "But that lie didn't last. You had to tell me another lie—and then another one."

"I'm sorry," said Benji.

"I forgive you," said his father. "And Jesus also forgives you. He gave his life so our sins could be forgiven."

"Does that mean all my lies are gone?" asked Benji.

"Yes, it means you don't have to tell more lies to cover up your past lies," said his father. "And it also means Jesus will help you tell the truth."

"How can he help?" asked Benji.

"When you remember that he loves and forgives you, you won't want to lie," said his father. "One lie causes another lie, and the lies keep on hurting you. But the truth lasts forever."

"But what if the truth hurts?" asked Benji.

"Jesus will help you with the hurt," said his father. "Lies hurt more than the truth, because each lie adds another hurt."

"I love you, Daddy," said Benji. "That's the truth!"

"I love you son," said his father. "And that's the truth too."

Some questions

Do you have a hard time believing people who have lied to you before?

Do some people not believe you because you have lied before?

How can you help someone who lies to you?

A prayer

Dear Jesus, forgive me when I tell a lie and help me to forgive and help those who lie to me. Amen.

But I Like to Talk

James 3:1-5

Cody was old enough to start kindergarten and he liked it. It was fun to be with the other children, and he liked to go off to school just like his big sisters. Of course, his sisters went to school all day and he went only half a day—but he still went to school.

After Cody had been in kindergarten a week his teacher took him off by himself for a talk.

"I can tell you like school," she said. "We want school to be fun, but we are also here to work. When it is time to work, you are not to talk to the other boys and girls."

"But I like to talk," said Cody.

"I can tell," said the teacher. "And you are fun to talk to. Talking is important. But schoolwork is important too. There is a time to study and a time to talk. Now is the time to study."

"OK," said Cody. On the way back to his desk Cody stopped at Joshua's desk.

"The teacher said I can't talk to you now, Josh," said Cody. "But we can talk at recess time."

Then he went to Brian's desk. "I can't talk to you now," he said to Brian. "The teacher said we have to work now."

Cody's teacher met him as he headed for Sarah's desk. "Cody!" she said. "Go to your desk! Do not talk to anyone!"

"But I have to tell my friends why I'm not talking to them," said Cody. "I don't want them to think I'm mad at them."

"I'm glad you are a friendly boy," his teacher said. "You are good at making friends. But you hurt your friends if you keep them from doing their work. I have to help you learn to do your work. Each time you talk when you should be studying

190

I'm going to have you sit over at that table by yourself. Then you can do your work. And your friends can do theirs."

Cody looked at the table far away from the other boys and girls. He did not want to be by himself. He opened his mouth to say that he would not talk. Then he stopped himself. He nodded his head, picked up his pencil, and started to do his work.

Some questions

Do you know when you should talk? And when you should listen?

Do you think you talk too much? Or not enough? Or just the right amount?

Do you say things that help others feel good?

A prayer

Dear God, thank you for giving me a way to talk. Help me say the right things. In Jesus' name. Amen.

Can We Buy a Lottery Ticket?
1 Timothy 6:6-10

(Note to parents: Perhaps your area does not have a state lottery yet. However, gambling is becoming more and more popular. Your children should become aware of it.)

Randy was in a store with his mother and father. As they were paying for the things they bought, he saw a sign about lottery tickets. It showed a person winning lots of money.

"Dad, can we buy a lottery ticket?" he asked. "It only costs a dollar."

"No, son," said his father. "I don't want to spend our money that way."

"But we might win lots of money," said Randy. "Then we'd be rich."

"Lotteries make very few people rich," said his father. "But they make many people poor."

"We won't be poor if we just buy one ticket," Randy said. By now the family had paid for their purchases and were walking toward the car.

"Let me show you how the lottery works," his father said. "Here is a dollar for you, one for your mother, and one for me." He gave each member of the family a dollar. "If we each bought a ticket, our money would be gone."

"But we might win!" said Randy.

"That's right," said his father. "But look what actually happens. The people who run the lottery keep one dollar and they divide the rest up among those who win. So, of our three dollars there are only two dollars left for prizes."

"But someone will get lots of money," said Randy.

"Sure!" said his father. "But all the people who buy tickets will lose more money than anyone will win. The people who run the lottery keep a big part of the money."

"But if we won, we would get some of it back," Randy said.

"But not all of it," his father said. "If we got our two dollars back, we couldn't even buy an ice-cream cone for each of us. But if we take the three dollars and buy ice-cream cones instead of lottery tickets, we can each have one."

"That's a good idea!" said Randy.

"OK, you lead the way to the ice-cream store," said his father.

Some questions

Do more people win or lose when they buy lottery tickets? If you want to give your money to someone else, could you do it in a better way than by buying a lottery ticket?

A prayer

Dear God, help us to enjoy the things we have, and help us to share them with others. In Jesus' name. Amen.

Why Can't I Vote?

Romans 13:1-5

Julie went with her mother to vote. She watched her mother sign the long list. Then she went with her mother into the voting booth. She stood real close to her when the curtain closed.

"Why can't I vote?" asked Julie as they left the building.

"Because you are not old enough," her mother answered.

"I'm old enough to go to school," said Julie.

"Yes," said her mother. "You are also old enough to help me take care of your baby sister. You're old enough to tie your shoes. But you are not old enough to vote."

"Why not?" asked Julie.

"To be able to vote you have to know about the people who are running for office," said her mother. "You have to know about government and what we need to help us live together."

"Do you know all that?" Julie asked.

"I try to vote very wisely," said her mother. "I read the newspaper and listen to the news on radio and TV."

"Did you vote for the right person?" asked Julie.

"I voted for the ones that I thought would do the best job," said her mother. "But not everyone will vote the same way I did. Others will think that someone else will do a better job."

"Will you be mad if the people you voted for don't win?" asked Julie.

"No," said her mother. "I'm glad other people voted too. And their vote is just as important as mine. I didn't vote just for the people who would help me the most. I thought about you and other people who can't vote. I want to elect people who will help you too."

"Do you like to vote?" asked Julie.

"Yes," said her mother. "When you grow up I hope you remember the times when you went with me to vote. I hope you will vote too."

"I will," said Julie. "But I'll only vote for people who will do good things."

Does your family talk about elections?
Do you think everyone should vote?
Do the people who vote help you?

A prayer

Dear God, help those who vote, and help those who are elected do their jobs. In Jesus' name. Amen.

Finish the Job
Colossians 3:23-24

"Hey, David!" his mother called, "I asked you to set the table."

"I did," said David as he turned on the TV.

"But you didn't finish the job," said his mother.

"It's as good as done," he answered.

"As-good-as is not enough," answered his mother. "Turn off the TV and get back in here!"

"It's all done," said David as he came back to the dining area. "See!"

"Yes," said his mother. "I see the knives, forks, and spoons all in one place. You are supposed to put them beside each plate. I also see only three glasses. How many are there in our family?"

"Five," he answered.

"Then we need five glasses," said his mother.

David got the two extra glasses and placed the silverware by each plate.

"That's a lot better," said his mother. "We'll be ready to eat in a few minutes, so don't turn on the TV again. Sit down and let's talk for a minute."

"What do we need to talk about?" asked David.

"What do you think?" asked his mother.

"About setting the table," answered David.

"No," said his mother. "That job is done and the table looks nice. Let's talk about finishing a job when you start it."

"Do we have to?" he asked.

"I've started the talk and I want to finish it," said his mother. "Do you know why it is important to finish a job when you have started it?"

"I guess because it's no good to do something halfway."

"That's right!" his mother said. "Some people get in the habit of starting all kinds of things and not finishing anything. Do you think you do that?"

"Sometimes," he said.

"Your teacher tells me you don't finish your homework," his mother said. "You started making a model car and you didn't finish it. But you *did* finish the book you were reading. And you *did* stay on your ball team all year."

"So I *do* finish some things," David said.

"Yes," said his mother, "and I'm glad. I just want to help you finish more of the things that you start. Maybe not everything—but at least most things."

"I'll finish eating dinner," he said, "if we can start to eat right away!"

Some questions

Do you finish most jobs that you start?

Why do you stop some things before they are finished?

If you are having trouble finishing something, who can help you?

A prayer

Dear God, help me to know what I can do and what I can't do, and help me to finish what I start. In Jesus' name. Amen.

She Loves You More Than Me

Genesis 37:3-4

"Let's go and play!" Rob said to his younger brother Rick.

"I don't want to play with you," answered Rick.

"Why not?" asked Rob.

"Because you're Mom's pet," said Rick. "She loves you more than me."

"What makes you think that?" asked Rob.

"Because she always spoils you," said Rick. "And you always get your way."

"She does *not* spoil me," yelled Rob. "I take care of myself."

"We were supposed to clean our room," said Rick. "Mom helped you do your part, but she didn't help me."

"I didn't know how to use the cleaner," said Rob. "Anyhow, she helped you make the beds."

"I made them myself!" said Rick. "All she did was fuss over them after I had done the work."

"Mom always fixes you special food," said Rob. "She doesn't do that for me."

"That's because I have allergies and can't eat some things," said Rick. "She gives you a bigger allowance than I get."

"That's because I'm older," said Rob. "When I was your age I didn't get as much as you do."

The two brothers glared at each other. Rob threw the ball in the air and caught it. After several throws he tossed the ball toward Rick, who caught it. Rick tossed it back.

"If we're going to play we had better go outside," said Rick, "or Mom will be mad at both of us."

"I thought you didn't want to play with me," said Rob.

"Well," said Rick. "Maybe Mom loves you more when you need it and me more when I need it."

"Yeah," said Rob. "That's the way it is."

Some questions

Do you think your parents or teachers treat some children better than others?

196

Do you think you sometimes get better treatment than others?

A prayer

Lord Jesus, help my parents to love me and also to love others. Help me to love all people. Amen.

God Loves You, Too
Matthew 28:16-20

"Hey, Todd," said his new friend Don, "my family is going on a picnic next Sunday and Mom said I could ask you to come with us. Do you want to come?"

"What time are you going?" asked Todd.

"We'll leave about nine o'clock," answered Don. "We'll get home before dark."

"I'm going to church and Sunday school," said Todd. "We don't get home from that until almost lunchtime."

"Wouldn't you rather go on a picnic?" Don asked.

"I like picnics," Todd said, "but I always go to church first."

"Why?" asked Don.

"Because I like what we do there," answered Todd.

"What do you do?" Don asked.

"Haven't you ever been to church?" asked Todd.

"No," answered Don, "my family doesn't go to church."

"Would you like to come with me?" Todd asked.

"I don't know," answered Don. "Why should I?"

"Because God loves you, too," answered Todd.

"How do you know God loves me?" Don asked.

"God says he loves everybody," Todd answered. "We learn about the things he does for us in Sunday school. You could come and learn about them too."

"Does your whole family go to church?" asked Don.

"Sure!" said Todd. "I like to sit in church with my mom and dad."

"Do you just sit there?" asked Don.

"No," said Todd, "we sing songs and pray. Sometimes I listen to the pastor preach and sometimes I think about other things."

"What do you think about in church?" Don asked.

"The same things you think about all the time," answered Todd. "Only you think about them and about Jesus at the same time."

"I thought Jesus watched you to see if you did something wrong," said Don.

"No," answered Todd, "Jesus is our friend. He likes to be with us, and I like to be with him. Do you want to come to church with us?"

"If I did," answered Don, "would your parents take us out to the park after church so we can eat with my family?"

"Sure!" said Todd.

Some questions

Do you know why you go to church?

Could you tell someone else how you feel about Jesus?

Do you know anyone who might like to go to church with you?

A prayer

Dear God, thank you for those who told me about you and your love for me. Help me to tell others. In Jesus' name. Amen.

Don't Leave Me Alone!
Psalm 27:1

"Why are you getting all dressed up?" Jason asked his mother.

"Because your father and I are going out to dinner," his mother answered.

"What should I wear?" asked Jason.

"You can wear what you have on," answered his mother, "because you're not going."

"I want to go with you," said Jason. "I'll be good."

"I know you're always good when we go out," said his mother. "But this is a special evening for your daddy and me to be by ourselves."

"I don't like being left alone," Jason said.

"You know we will not leave you alone," said his mother. "Jenny will be your baby-sitter."

"I don't like staying with a baby-sitter," said Jason. "I'd rather be with you."

"I like being with you too," his mother said. "I spent time with you all by yourself today. Your daddy spent time just with you last Saturday. He and I also need some time to be by ourselves."

"I can't go to sleep when you're not here," Jason said. "I'm afraid that you won't come back."

"Of course we will come back!" said his mother. "We love you very much. When we come home, we always come to your room and check to see that you are OK."

"Do you like having me with you?" asked Jason.

"Of course we like having you with us!" answered his mother. "We take you along when we do things that include children. Tonight we are going to do adult things."

"Will Jenny read me a story?" asked Jason.

"Go and find the book you want her to read," said his mother, "and I'm sure she will read it to you."

Some questions

Do you like to stay with a baby-sitter?

Do you like to be alone with one of your parents sometimes?

Do you think parents like to be by themselves sometimes?

A prayer

Dear God, help me when I am afraid. When my mother and father go away, always help them to come back safely. In Jesus' name. Amen.

Clean Your Room

Colossians 3:20-21

"Tony, I told you that you had to clean your room before you could watch TV," his mother said.

"But I did clean it!" said Tony.

"It still looks like a mess to me," said his mother.

"You should have seen it before I cleaned it!" answered Tony.

"No, I want to see it after you clean it," said his mother. "Turn off the TV. I'll go with you to show you what it means to clean a room."

Tony and his mother went to his bedroom.

"First of all," his mother said, "what are those clothes doing on your bed?"

"Those are clean clothes," said Tony. "I was going to wear them, but I changed my mind. You can't say they make the room dirty; they're clean."

"What about the socks under the bed?" asked his mother. "And the shirt on the floor?"

"Those are dirty clothes," said Tony. "But they're not very dirty."

"Look at the dust on your dresser," said his mother. "You've even got dirty dishes in here. And look—there's half an apple that is starting to rot."

"Why are you so fussy about everything?" asked Tony. "I want my room to be comfortable."

"I'm not that fussy," said his mother. "I don't mind having your games and toys around; I can stand a little mess. But your room cannot have filth in it and you have to straighten it up once in a while."

"When Grandma was here she told me that cleanliness was next to godliness," said Tony. "Is that in the Bible?"

"No, that's not in the Bible," said his mother. "That's only what your grandmother thinks."

"She said I was a bad boy if I had a messy room," said Tony.

"No, you are not a bad boy," said his mother. "You are a good boy and God loves you even if you have a messy room.

I love you too. I care about you so much that I want to teach you how to take care of your things."

"OK," said Tony. "I'll pick this stuff up."

"I'll help you this time," said his mother. "I want you to see how nice your room can look. Then you can keep it that way."

Some questions

What do you do to keep your room neat?
Do you do more to mess up your home or to clean it up?
Who is responsible for keeping your home clean?

A prayer

Thank you, God, for our home and for our rooms. Help us to enjoy our home and take care of it so that others can enjoy it too. In Jesus' name. Amen.

I've Got to Finish This Job
Titus 3:14

"Daddy, can you play with me now?" Tim asked his father, who was painting the garage.

"Not now, son," said his father. "I've got to finish this job."

"Can we play after you finish this wall?" asked Tim. "No," said his father, "I want to finish the whole garage this afternoon."

Tim went into the house for a little while. Then he came back and stood at the bottom of the ladder, watching his father paint.

"Can I help paint?" he asked.

"I've got something you can do," said his father. He came down the ladder and went into the house. Soon he came back with a bucket of water and a clean brush.

201

"Here, Tim," the father said, "you can paint the driveway while I paint the garage."

Tim was happy to be working with his father. He used the brush to put water on the driveway, and he watched as it turned from white to grey.

When Tim's bucket was empty, he ran into the house to fill it again. When he returned most of the driveway was white again. So he started over. But the hot sun dried up the water soon after he put it on the driveway. Tim painted the same area a third time. He started to cry.

"What's the matter, son?" asked his father.

"I can't get my job done!" said Tim. "See, I work and work and it doesn't stay the way I want it. You get your work done, but I can't finish mine."

"Don't worry, Tim!" his father said as he came down the ladder. "You've made the driveway look clean, so your job is done."

"It is?" asked Tim.

"Yes, it is," said his father. "And mine is too. I'll do the other side of the garage next Saturday. Let's go and play."

Some questions

Why do children like to do the same things as their parents do?

Do children have to be able to do things as well as adults?

Some people don't do as much as they should. Can some also try to do too much?

A prayer

Dear God, help me to know what I can do well, and help me to enjoy doing it. In Jesus' name. Amen.

Can You Say It Another Way?

Ephesians 4:26-27

The second-grade class was out on the playground for recess. Adam grabbed Eric's hat and threw it to another boy. Soon the boys were throwing the hat back and forth to each other as Eric chased them and tried to get his hat back. Eric became angry.

"Give me my hat!" he yelled. "If you don't give it to me, I'll kill you!"

Mrs. Harris heard the yelling and saw what had happened. She asked for Eric's hat and gave it back to him. Eric was still angry. His face was red and his fists were clenched.

"The other boys were wrong when they took your hat," said Mrs. Harris. "I will talk to them, but first I want to talk to you."

"They tease me all the time," said Eric. "I get so mad I'm going to kill them."

"I can understand why you get angry," said Mrs. Harris. "They shouldn't tease you. Can I help you to show your anger in another way?"

"They all gang up on me," Eric said. "That's not fair!"

"No, it's not fair," his teacher said. "But what you said was not good either. Do you remember what you said?"

"I said I was going to kill them," said Eric.

"Do you know what that means?" asked Mrs. Harris.

"Yes," Eric said.

"Did you mean it?" Mrs. Harris asked.

"I was mad at them," said Eric. "They took my hat."

"They were wrong," said Mrs. Harris. "I will talk to them. But what you said was wrong too."

"I had a right to get mad," said Eric.

"Maybe so," Mrs. Harris said. "But your anger didn't help. The other boys would have no fun teasing you if you didn't get angry."

"But they make me mad," said Eric.

"Even when you are angry, you do not have to say you will kill someone," said his teacher. "That makes what you did as

bad as what they did. You can get rid of your anger another way."

"How?" Eric asked.

"You could tell me what happened and I would help you," Mrs. Harris said. "Doing something else like playing a game, kicking a ball, or running also helps to get rid of anger. Even just talking helps sometimes. Do you feel better now?"

"Yes," said Eric.

"Good!" said Mrs. Harris. "Now I want to go and talk to Adam and the other boys."

Some questions

Do children sometimes like to tease others to make them angry?

What are some things you can do that will not hurt you or others when you are angry?

Should you try to make others angry?

A prayer

Dear Jesus, help me to control my temper, and forgive me when I say bad things. Amen.

Will the Devil Get Me?
Matthew 4:1-11

Jason and his mother were in their pastor's office. His mother had made an appointment so they could talk to the pastor. Jason liked the pastor, but he had never been in his office before.

"Jason is worried about something," his mother told the pastor. "I told him he should ask you about it because you are his friend."

"What's bothering you, Jason?" the pastor asked.

"I'm afraid the devil will get me," said Jason.

"Why do you think the devil will get you?" asked the pastor.

"Sometimes I say things I shouldn't say," Jason said. "And sometimes I get mad and hit someone."

"Do you know that Jesus loves you and forgives you?" asked the pastor.

"One of my friends said that if I do something wrong the devil will get me," said Jason.

"Do you know what your friend meant by that?" asked the pastor.

"He said the devil might make me fall down and break my nose," said Jason. "Or maybe my mother would get sick."

"Let me tell you something about the devil," said the pastor. "The devil only has power over people because they sin. And Jesus died to take all our sins away. God loves you and helps you. He will protect you from the devil and every bad thing."

"Then why does my friend tell me the devil will get me?" asked Jason.

"Maybe someone tried to scare your friend by telling him about the devil," said the pastor. "Why not help him by telling him about Jesus?"

"I could tell him that Jesus is on his side and will keep him safe from the devil," said Jason.

"Yes, you could!" said the pastor.

Some questions

Do you have to be afraid of the devil?
Can God help you when you are afraid of something?
How can you help other people know that God loves them?

A prayer

Thank you, Jesus, for taking away my sins. Protect me from all bad things. Amen.

Why Can You Tell Me What to Do?

Ephesians 6:1-3

"Go and change your shirt, Paul!" said his mother. "You can't wear that to school."

"But I want to wear this shirt today," said Paul.

"That shirt has a hole in the back," said his mother, "and it's dirty. Go and put on a clean shirt."

"Why can you tell me what to do?" asked Paul.

"Because I'm your mother," she answered.

"But it's my shirt and I'm the one who wears it," said Paul.

"I don't have time to argue with you," said his mother. "Change that shirt right now. We'll talk about it this evening."

Paul could tell by his mother's tone of voice that he had better do what she said. He was angry, but he changed the shirt.

When he came home that afternoon, his mother was waiting for him.

"Did you have a good day at school?" she asked.

"Kind of," he answered.

"We didn't get to finish our talk this morning," said his mother. "I think we should talk now."

"Do we have to?" asked Paul.

"Yes, we do," said his mother. "You wanted to know why I have a right to tell you what to do."

"I don't think it's fair for you to tell me what to wear, what to eat, and what I have to do," said Paul.

"I don't decide everything for you," said his mother. "The older you get, the more you can decide for yourself."

"I think I'm big enough to decide what I can wear," said Paul.

"I do let you decide sometimes," said his mother. "But when you decide to wear a dirty shirt with a hole in it, I have to help you make a better decision."

"But will I always have to do what you want me to do?"

"No," said his mother, "you have to learn how to decide what is best for you. I have to help you to learn how to decide for yourself. I know you will make some mistakes—we all do. But I want to help you as much as I can."

"Can I decide what I get for a snack now?" asked Paul.

"Let's try it," said his mother. "What do you want?"

"Three cookies," said Paul, "and an apple."

"Fine!" said his mother.

"What if I would have said six cookies and no apple?" asked Paul.

"You'd better stick with your first choice!" said his mother.

Some questions

What choices do you make for yourself?
What choices do your parents make for you?
Who else makes choices for you?

A prayer

Dear God, help me to make good choices, and help me to listen to those who try to guide me. In Jesus' name. Amen.

I'll Get Even
Matthew 5:38-42

Glenna was lying on the floor drawing a picture. It was part of her homework for school. The phone rang and her brother Chuck ran through the room to answer it. He stepped on her picture and tore it.

"Look what you did to my picture!" Glenna yelled.

Chuck did not pay any attention to her. He was talking to his friend on the phone. Glenna took the torn picture to her mother.

"Look what Chuck did to my picture!" she said. "He ruined it. Now I'll have to start over again."

"I'll talk to him about it," said his mother.

"That won't do any good," said Glenna. "He never listens. I'll get even with him. I'm going to tear some of his baseball cards in two."

"How will that help?" asked her mother.

"It will teach him a lesson," Glenna said. "He ruined my picture."

"Chuck was wrong when he stepped on your homework," said her mother. "But wouldn't you be wrong if you tore his pictures?"

"I've got a right to get even," said Glenna.

"No, you don't," her mother said. "The only way you can get even is to do something wrong too. Then you are acting just as badly as he is."

"But he deserves it," said Glenna.

"If you tear his pictures, he will do something else to get even with you," said her mother. "Then you'll do something to get even with him. That can keep going for a long time."

"Then what should I do?" asked Glenna.

"Let's talk to your brother and let him know that he has done something wrong," said her mother. "Then he can help you get started again. Instead of you doing something bad to him, let's ask him to do something good for you."

"That's a good idea!" said Glenna. "Where did you learn that?"

"From Jesus," said her mother.

Some questions

Why do people want to get even when someone hurts them?
Does getting even ever solve a problem?
Is it better to get even or to forgive?

A prayer

Dear Jesus, thank you for forgiving me when I do something wrong. Help me to forgive everyone who hurts me. Amen.

Do You Want to Be Like Jane?

Ephesians 5:6-11

"Cindy," called her mother, "it's time for you to go to bed."

"I don't want to go yet," answered Cindy.

"Tomorrow is a school day," said her mother. "Run and brush your teeth and I'll be in to hear your prayers."

"Jane doesn't have to go to bed this early," said Cindy. Jane lived with her family in the house next door.

"And Jane is five years older than you are," said her mother.

"Oh, hell!" said Cindy.

"Cindy! Why do you say something like that?" asked her mother.

"That's what Jane says," said Cindy.

"I'm sorry Jane talks that way," said her mother. "But I don't want you to talk that way. I think I see a problem here that we should discuss. Do you want to be like Jane?"

"I don't know," said Cindy.

"I've noticed that you often do and say things lately because that's what Jane does," said her mother.

"I want to be like Jane," said Cindy.

"What is it about Jane that you like?" asked her mother.

"She has lots of friends," said Cindy. "And she's like a person on television."

"Is there anything about Jane that you don't like?" asked her mother.

"No," said Cindy. "I want to be just like her."

"We all look to other people to be examples for us," said her mother. "There are some good things about Jane that I hope you can follow. But Jane does some things I would not want you to do."

"Like what?" asked Cindy.

"Jane uses bad language," said her mother. "Jane also lies to her mother and father. She got into serious trouble because she sneaked out her window one night. The police brought her home."

"But she had fun," said Cindy. "She told me she did."

"She may have had fun, but she made many other people unhappy," said her mother. "Is that a good way to have fun?"

"No," said Cindy. "But Jane will talk to me, and most older girls won't."

"Yes, that's something good about Jane," said her mother. "I hope you will also be kind to younger children. But I hope you do not do many of the other things Jane does."

"I think I understand," said Cindy.

"Good!" said her mother. "I'm glad we had this talk."

Some questions

Who are some people you want to be like?
Who is a good example for you to follow?
Who is a bad example for you to follow?

A prayer

Dear God, thank you for other people. Give me good friends, and help me be a good friend to others. In Jesus' name. Amen.

Can We Pray Here?
Matthew 6:5-6

The Thompson family went out for dinner at a restaurant. The children enjoyed looking at the menu and telling the waitress what they wanted to eat. Then they nibbled on the breadsticks in a basket as they waited for the food.

"Here she comes!" said Danny as he saw the waitress come toward their table.

"And just in time," said Mr. Thompson. "I'm hungry."

The waitress put a plate in front of each member of the family. Danny picked up one of the french fries and ate it.

"Wait," said Nancy. "We haven't said our prayer yet."

"Are we going to pray here?" asked Danny.

"We always pray before our meals," said Mrs. Thompson.

"But we learned in Sunday school that Jesus said we should pray in private," said Danny. "He said we shouldn't show off when we pray."

"Do you think we would be showing off if we prayed here?" asked his father.

"Everyone will see us," said Danny.

"It would be showing off if we stood up and said our prayer very loud," said Nancy. "But we can pray just like we do at home."

"But people will still see us," said Danny.

"So what!" said Nancy. "I remember something from Sunday school too. The Bible says that when Daniel wanted to pray he stood at a window. He wanted people to know he believed in God. He didn't try to hide his prayer, and we don't have to either."

"I'm glad you two remember your Sunday school lessons so well," said their mother. "I know we're all eager to eat."

"So let's pray!" said Danny. "But let's not all hold hands like we do at home."

"OK," said Mr. Thompson, "let's say our prayer together."

Some questions

Do you think the Thompson family should have said their prayer in a restaurant?

Why do people pray before they eat?

Could God hear you if you only thought your prayer instead of saying it out loud?

A prayer

Dear God, thank you for hearing my prayers when I say them, think them, and sing them. In Jesus' name. Amen.

I Think Julie Is Dumb

Matthew 7:1-5

Cheryl and her mother were planning her birthday party. Her mother said she could have five friends stay overnight with her. Cheryl was trying to decide which friends to invite.

"I know I want Amy and Susie," said Cheryl.

"Would you like to invite Julie?" asked her mother.

"No," said Cheryl, "I think Julie is dumb."

"Why do you say that?" her mother asked.

"Because she does dumb things," Cheryl said.

"Does she think she does dumb things?" asked her mother.

"No, but I do," said Cheryl.

"What does she do that you think is dumb?" her mother asked.

"Well," Cheryl said, "for one thing, she takes music lessons."

"What kind of lessons?" asked her mother.

"She plays the flute," said Cheryl. "And she practices every day. That's dumb."

"Maybe she likes to play the flute," said her mother.

"Think of all the other things she could be doing," Cheryl said. "She could play outside, she could watch TV, or she could go skating."

"You like to spend your extra time roller skating, don't you?" said her mother.

"Sure!" said Cheryl. "It's fun."

"It's fun for you," said her mother. "Playing the flute is fun for Julie. Does Julie think you are dumb because you like to play basketball?"

"I don't know," said Cheryl.

"You might think about that," said her mother. "Each of us likes different things. I'm glad not everyone plays the flute. But I'm also glad not everyone plays basketball."

"Do you think I'm dumb because I like to play basketball?" asked Cheryl.

"No," said her mother. "But then I don't think Julie is dumb because she likes to play the flute."

213

"OK," said Cheryl, "let's invite her to my party. She tells funny stories about her big brother."

Some questions

Do you want all your friends to be exactly like you?
Do you like some things that your friends don't like?
Do your friends like some things that you don't like?

A prayer

Dear God, thank you for giving me some special things that I like. Help me to understand and love people who are different from me. In Jesus' name. Amen.

I'm Going to Tell on You
Colossians 3:12-17

"I'm going to tell on you," Joel said to his brother Dennis.

"What did I do?" asked Dennis.

"Mom said we had to come right home from school," said Joel. "I saw you stop and talk to your friends."

"I got home at the same time you did," said Dennis.

"But I came straight home," Joel said. "You stopped and talked to someone."

"Then why did I get home at the same time you did?" asked Dennis.

"Because I walked slower," said Joel. "But Mom didn't say that I couldn't walk slow. I came straight home."

"You're a tattletale," said Dennis. "You just want to get me in trouble."

"You told on me last week," Joel said.

"What did I say?" asked Dennis.

"You told Mom that I threw away my homework," said Joel.

"But you *did* throw it away," said Dennis. "And you lied when you said you didn't."

"But you were a tattletale," Joel said.

"I told on you because you did something wrong and told a lie," Dennis said. "You want to tell on me just to get me in trouble."

"Then you won't tell on me the next time?" said Joel.

"Go ahead and tell Mom whatever you want," said Dennis. "She'll know that you're just trying to get even with me."

"No, she won't," Joel said. "She'll give you the same punishment she gave me."

"She made you do your homework over again," Dennis said. "I don't have any homework to do."

"Well," said Joel, "she'll think of something."

"I think you'll look dumb if you tell Mom that I didn't come straight home," said Dennis.

"I might tell—and I might not," said Joel.

Some questions

Do you think Dennis should have told on Joel for throwing away his homework?

Do you think Joel should tell on Dennis for talking to his friends on the way home from school?

How do you know when you should tell on others and when you should not?

A prayer

Forgive us when we do something wrong, and help us help others when they do something wrong. Amen.

Were You Surprised When I Was Born?

Jeremiah 1:4-8

"Your daddy and I had a surprise last night," Teddy's mother told him. "Your Uncle Walt phoned. He and Aunt Grace had a baby girl. We didn't even know they were expecting a baby."

"Were Uncle Walt and Aunt Grace surprised too?" asked Teddy.

"They're glad," said his mother, "but they weren't surprised. They knew they were expecting a baby. They just didn't tell us."

"Were you surprised when I was born?" Teddy asked.

"We were very happy, but we weren't surprised," his mother said. "We had prayed and asked God to give us a baby."

"How did you know you were going to have me?" asked Teddy.

"When I found out I was pregnant, we knew we would have a baby," said his mother. "We had nine months to get ready for your birth."

"Did you know I would be a boy?" Teddy asked.

"No," answered his mother. "We didn't know exactly what day you would be born, and we didn't know whether God would give us a boy or girl. So we had *some* surprises."

"Were you glad that I was a boy?" he asked.

"Yes, but we would also have been glad if our baby would have been a girl," said his mother. "While we were waiting for you, Daddy and I would talk about you. We loved you even before you were born."

"Where was I then?" asked Teddy.

"You were inside me," his mother told him.

"Why was I there?" he asked.

"Because you had to grow big enough to be born," said his mother. "You needed to be kept very warm and safe. You were connected to my body until you were big enough to be born and to grow on your own."

"I'm glad you took good care of me," said Teddy.

"Your Daddy and I will still take good care of you," his mother said. "But every day you get a little bit bigger and you learn a little bit more about taking care of yourself."

"I can put on my own shoes!" said Teddy.

"And you can give your mother a big hug!" she said.

Some questions

When did your parents start loving you?

When did you start loving your parents?

As you grow older, can you show your love to your parents in different ways?

A prayer

Thank you, God, for giving me to my mother and father and for giving them to me. In Jesus' name. Amen.

A Time to Be Quiet
Habakkuk 2:20

It was Sunday afternoon. Maria was sitting on her father's lap.

"Did you like being in church this morning?" her father asked.

"It was kind of long," said Maria.

"Sometimes it *is* a long time for children," said her father, "but we have a lot of things to do when we worship. I like to sit with you and your mother in church."

"I like to be with you," Maria said. "You held my hand today and Mommy let me keep her purse on my lap."

"That was nice," her father said. "But I would like to ask you to be more quiet in church. We usually like it when you talk, but talking in church causes problems."

"I didn't say anything bad," said Maria.

"No, you didn't," said her father. "But you talked during the prayers."

"But God can hear our prayers anyway," said Maria. "He can hear our prayers even when we don't say them out loud."

"That's right, and I'm glad you know how God hears our prayers," her father said. "But the problem is not God. In church we are praying together. If you make noise, other people can't hear what the pastor is saying and can't join in praying together."

"Did I sin when I talked?" asked Maria.

"It's not a sin to talk," said her father. "Jesus not only forgives us when we do something wrong; he also helps us do right things. Jesus loves all the other people as well as you, and he can help you think about the other people so that they can worship too."

"It's all right to make noise sometimes," said Maria.

"Of course it is!" her father said. "We can praise God when we laugh and sing. There is a time to make noise and have fun. And there is a time to be quiet and have fun."

"You think church is a place to be quiet," Maria said.

"Yes, most of the time," said her father. "And I still think it's fun to sit with you."

Some questions

Do you like to be with other people in church?

Do you know that other people like to have you with them in church?

If people are going to pray together, why is it important for them to be quiet?

A prayer

Dear God, thank you for all the others who worship Jesus with me. Help me enjoy them, and help them enjoy me. Amen.

My Father Gave Me This

2 Timothy 1:5-7

Mark and his father were cleaning the closet in the guest room to make more room to store some suitcases.

"Look at this!" said Mark's father. "Here's a box of things that my father gave me."

"What's in it?" asked Mark.

"Lots of things," said his father. "Here's my dad's birth certificate. He weighed six pounds and four ounces when he was born."

"It looks old," said Mark.

"It's 70 years old," his father said, "because that's how old my father would be if he were still alive."

"What else is in the box?" asked Mark.

"Here's a picture of my dad when he was your age," said his father. "You look like him. Here is an arrowhead that he found on his father's farm. He gave it to me many years ago."

"Your dad gave you a lot of neat things," said Mark.

"He also gave me a lot of things that aren't in this box," his father said.

"Where are they?" asked Mark.

"They are in me," said his father.

"In you?" said Mark. "That's funny!"

"My father gave me a sense of humor," said Mark's father. "He also taught me how to enjoy life."

"How?" asked Mark.

"He was older than most fathers when I was born, and he was in poor health," said his father. "He couldn't play sports with me and take me on hikes. But he taught me how to let other people love me, and he taught me how to love other people."

"How'd he do that?" asked Mark.

"He'd hug me and tell me that he loved me," his father said, "just like I do you."

"Is that all?" Mark asked.

"No, he told me about Jesus," said his father. "He knew Jesus loved him. When I did something bad, he would always say that, since Jesus still loved me, he would too."

"You said that to me last week!" said Mark.

"I did, didn't I?" his father said. "Do you think you will say that to your children too?"

"I might," said Mark.

Some questions

Think about your family: What important things are your parents giving to you?

What important things are you giving to your parents?

What else would you like to receive from each other?

A prayer

Dear God, thank you for my parents who teach me about Jesus. Help me to remember all that Jesus has done so that I can teach my children about him too. Amen.

I Don't Like Daddy Tonight
Proverbs 23:29-35

"Why are you making me go to bed early tonight?" Eddie asked his mother.

"You don't have to go to bed," said his mother. "Just stay in your room and keep quiet."

"You want me to stay away from Daddy because he's drinking, don't you?" asked Eddie.

"Yes," said his mother.

"I don't like Daddy when he drinks," said Eddie. "He thinks he's funny. But he's mean and dumb."

"I'm sorry your father acts that way when he drinks," his mother said. "I want you to love your father. He is a good man. But it's the alcohol that causes him to act that way."

"Then why does he drink?" asked Eddie.

"Because he can't control himself," said his mother. "The alcohol makes him think in strange ways. We need to understand that he is not a bad person. He has let alcohol take control of him. He needs our help."

"Then why don't we help him?" Eddie asked.

"That's exactly what we're going to do, Eddie," his mother said. "But it's not going to be easy. I've been talking to our pastor and to a doctor to see what we can do. We're all going to have to work together to help your father understand that he has a problem and that he will have to get help for it."

"I'm afraid of him when he's like this," said Eddie.

"I know, son," said his mother. "I want you to know I will take care of you. I will not let him hurt you."

"Tomorrow he'll pretend he didn't say those bad things to me tonight," Eddie said.

"I know," answered his mother. "But we must never lie for him or lie to him. We are not doing anything wrong. We do not have to lie."

"I'm glad you don't get drunk, Mom," said Eddie.

"I am too!" she answered

Some questions

Does the use of alcohol cause problems in your family?

Do you know other families that are sad because someone drinks too much alcohol?

How can you help people who drink too much alcohol?

A prayer

Dear God, please help all people who drink too much alcohol. Help them to ask you and others for help. Be with their families. In Jesus' name. Amen.

Her House Is Nicer Than Ours

James 2:1-4

"Mary's mother phoned to invite you to spend Friday night with them," Jean's mother told her. "Isn't that nice?"

"I don't want to go," said Jean.

"You don't?" said her mother. "I thought you would be glad to go. You had such a good time when you stayed with her before. Her mother said they liked having you as a guest."

"I don't feel like going again," said Jean.

"Why not?" asked her mother.

"Because I can't ask Mary to come to my house," answered Jean.

"But you can ask her to our home," said her mother. "I'd be glad to have her stay with us."

"But our house isn't as nice as hers," said Jean.

"What do you mean?" her mother asked.

"Mary's house is real fancy," Jean said. "Ours is plain, and we have old furniture."

"But this is our home," said her mother. "We are happy here. We don't need a fancy house and new furniture to be happy."

"But Mary is happy in her home too," said Jean. "I would be embarrassed to have her come here."

"Do you like Mary only because she has a beautiful home?" asked her mother.

"No," Jean said, "she's my best friend at school."

"Do you think she won't like you if she comes to our house?" her mother asked.

"I don't know," said Jean.

"If she is your friend at school, don't you think she likes you because of who you are?" asked her mother.

"I guess so," Jean said.

"Would you like her any less if she lived in a house that wasn't as nice as ours?" her mother asked.

"No, I wouldn't," said Jean. "Instead of staying at her house Friday night, could I invite Mary here?"

"You sure can!" said her mother. "We'll have a good time."

Some questions

Do you think Mary will spend the night with Jean?

Do you like people because of who they are or because of what they have?

Do you think other people like you because of who you are or because of what you have?

A prayer

Dear God, help me to be a friend to all other people, and help other people to be my friends. In Jesus' name. Amen.

I'm Sorry I Said That

James 4:11-12

Teri and her mother were baking. They were having fun together.

"I like to help you, Mom," Teri said.

"And I like to have you help me," said her mother. "While we're together, there's something I want to talk to you about."

"What?" asked Teri.

"Remember last Saturday when we had a problem?" her mother said. "I said something I should not have said."

The smile left Teri's face. She looked sad. "I don't want to talk about that again," said Teri. "I said I was sorry and you said you forgave me."

"I did forgive you," said her mother. "Now I want you to forgive me."

"Why should I forgive you?" asked Teri. "I was wrong. I said I am sorry that I told a lie."

"That's what I want to talk to you about," her mother said. "Yes, you were wrong because you told a lie. But I forgave you and we know that Jesus forgives you. But I was wrong when I called you a liar."

"I did tell a lie," said Teri.

"Yes, you did," said her mother. "And I'm glad I corrected you because I don't want you to tell more lies. But I should not have called you a liar."

"It made me feel bad," Teri said.

"I know," her mother said. "That's why I'm telling you I am sorry. When I called you a liar, it sounded as though you always lie—and you don't. You told a lie. There is a difference."

"I tell the truth almost all the time," said Teri.

"I know you do, dear," said her mother. "And I want to help you to tell the truth all the time. That's why I don't want you to think of yourself as a liar. You are a good person to be with. I love you very much."

"Thanks, Mom," said Teri. "I like being with you."

Some questions

Have you called people bad names that you did not mean?

Do you think others have called you names that they did not mean?

Is there a difference between correcting someone and finding fault with someone?

A prayer

Dear Jesus, forgive me when I call other people bad names and help me to forgive others when they make me feel bad. Amen.

Why Did You Do That?

Ephesians 4:20-24

Nathan and Tommy were walking home from school. They were playing a game as they walked. One boy would throw a rock far ahead of them. The other would toss another rock and try to make it land as close as possible to the first one. Then they would walk to where the rocks had landed and throw them again.

As they were walking along, they passed an empty house. It was Nathan's turn to throw the rock first. He picked the rock up and threw it toward the house. The rock hit a window and broke it.

"Why did you do that?" asked Tommy.

"I wanted to see if I could throw the rock that far," said Nathan.

"But you didn't have to break a window," said Tommy. "You could have thrown it at something else."

"It doesn't make any difference," Nathan said. "No one lives in that house."

"But the house still belongs to someone," Tommy said. "There's a 'For Sale' sign in the yard."

"They can pay for a new window," said Nathan.

"I don't think that's fair," said Tommy. "And I think there's something wrong with you."

"What's wrong with me?" Nathan said.

"Why would you want to break something for no reason?" asked Tommy.

"I don't know," said Nathan.

"You ought to think about it," said Tommy. "If you just break things for fun, you're strange."

"Why are you making such a big deal out of it?"

"Because you're my friend," Tommy said. "I don't think you should break things like that."

"OK, I won't do it again," said Nathan.

"If you really want to learn a lesson, you should pay for the window you just broke," said Tommy.

"How can I? I don't know who owns that house."

"There's a phone number on the sign," Tommy said.

"You think I should phone them and say I broke the window?" asked Nathan.

"Yes, I do!" said Tommy.

Some questions

Do you think Nathan should pay for the window?

Have you ever broken something on purpose for no reason?

Have you seen others break things on purpose?

A prayer

Dear Father in heaven, thank you for all the things you have made for us. Help us to take good care of what we own and what others own. In Jesus' name. Amen.

Why Are You Sad?
1 Thessalonians 5:9-11

Jennifer noticed her mother sitting by herself on the back porch. Her mother had been sitting there for a long time.

"Are you sad?" Jennifer asked her mother.

"Yes, I guess I am," she said as she took Jennifer on her lap.

"Why are you sad?" Jennifer asked.

"I don't know," said her mother. "I guess I was sad without even thinking about it. I'm glad you asked."

"Are you sad about me?" asked Jennifer. "Have I done something wrong?"

"Oh, no," her mother said as she kissed her. "You are a joy to me."

"Are you sick?" Jennifer asked.

"No, I feel all right," said her mother. "Sometimes I just feel a little blue. There's nothing wrong. I know I'll feel better soon."

"What will make you better?" asked Jennifer.

"You are helping right now," her mother said. "It makes me feel good to hold you in my lap."

"I like that too," said Jennifer. "I don't like to see you sad."

"I'm sorry if I've made you worry," said her mother. "When some people are around, I pretend I'm happy when I'm not. I feel so close to you so I don't pretend when I'm around you."

"When I was sick, we prayed to Jesus and asked him to help me," Jennifer said.

"Yes," her mother said, "and I know that Jesus helped. Sometimes when I am sad, I forget to pray. Thank you for reminding me to ask for God's help."

"You told me God is with me even when I hurt," said Jennifer.

"That's right!" said her mother. "And he is with me even when I am sad. You have helped me, Jennifer. Let's go for a walk!"

Some questions

When you are sad, can you ask someone for help? Whom?
When someone else is sad, can you help them? How?
Do you think everyone has times when they are sad?

A prayer

Dear God, help me when I feel sad and lonely. Send someone to be my friend. And send me to be the friend of someone else who is sad. In Jesus' name. Amen.

Should I Tell?
Psalm 32:3-5

Dear Susie,

Sorry I've been acting weird lately. I know I said nasty things to you yesterday. I'm worried about something and I've just got to talk to someone about it. After you read this letter, tear it up and flush it. Promise?

You know Jerry and Dan. They're in my class at school, and I brought them along to the party at your house last Christmas. I thought they were good guys, and they really are my best friends at school.

Well, anyway, the Saturday before last we were all going to Dan's house. We walked past a house where the garage door was left open. There were no cars around. Jerry said that he bet no one was home. Dan said someone might be. So they rang the door bell and no one answered.

They went into the garage. I went along because I didn't know what they were going to do. They found a bike and some Ping-Pong paddles and balls. They took them. I didn't touch a thing. Jerry took the Ping-Pong stuff to his house. They hid the bike in the alley by Dan's house.

I know it was stealing and I know that's a sin. I'm telling you because we go to church together and I hope you can understand. I don't want to steal and do wrong things. I told them they ought to take the things back. But they wouldn't do it.

Then I told them that if they didn't take it back I'd tell the cops. They laughed at me and told me that I was with them and that I would be arrested too.

Do you think I would be?

I don't want to go to jail. And I don't want Jerry and Dan to go to jail either. But they did something wrong and I think they should take the things back. What do you think?

Please don't talk to me on the phone about this. If Mom or Dad knew about it, they wouldn't let me play with Jerry and Dan anymore.

I've never been in a mess like this before. Can you help me? Remember, tear this letter up after you read it.

Matt

Some questions

How would you help Matt?

If you were Matt, whom could you have asked for help?

228

If you were Matt, what would you say to Jerry and Dan?

A prayer

Jesus, forgive me when I am wrong, and help me to show others that they can confess and be forgiven too. Amen.

You've Got to Do Something
Psalm 32:8-11

(Note: This devotion is a reply to the previous one. Before you read this, remind the family of the letter that Matt wrote to Susie in the last devotion.)

Dear Matt,

I got your letter. Don't worry, I read it and tore it up. No one will ever find even a piece of it.

I wondered why you were acting the way you were. I thought you were mad at me or something. I wondered what I had done wrong. So I'm glad you told me.

Wow! I don't know what I'd do if I were you. I'm glad you didn't steal that stuff. Do you know if Jerry and Dan have done this before? Maybe they steal all the time. If they get away with stealing the bike and things, I'll bet they'll do it again.

Don't do something dumb like trying to take the bike back by yourself. They might catch you taking it back and think you were stealing it. Then you'd be in real trouble.

I don't think Jerry and Dan are very good friends. Friends don't do things like that. And if friends do something wrong, they'll listen to you and try to make it right. I'm glad you know that it was wrong. If you want to be their friend, you've got to help them before they get into really big trouble.

I'm glad you wrote that note to me. Maybe you can tell someone else. Could you tell your teachers at school? Teachers work with lots of kids. Sometimes they know what to do.

Or why not tell your mom and dad? They might be mad at you at first because you shouldn't have gone into the garage. But after they yell at you, they'll help you. Mine always do.

Or maybe you should tell Jerry and Dan's parents. Have you been to their house? They might be nice people who would want to help their kids. My parents would want someone to tell them—and I bet yours would too.

You've got to do something. You sound scared to me, and you're acting funny. You didn't do anything wrong and you're all worried. But I'm sure you'll find the right thing to do.

Let's talk about this after church on Sunday, OK?

Susie

Some questions

Do you think Susie helped Matt?
What do you think Matt will do?
What would you do if you were Matt?

A prayer

Dear God, thank you for helping me when I need it. Help me to help others. In Jesus' name. Amen.

I Don't Like Adults

Luke 17:1-4

"How old are you?" Gary asked his baby-sitter.

"I'm 16," Ellen answered.

"Are you an adult or a kid?" asked Gary.

"Your parents treat me like an adult," said Ellen. "My parents treat me like a kid."

"I think you're a kid," said Gary, "because I don't like adults."

"Why don't you like adults?" asked Ellen.

"They tell me not to do things that they do," Gary said.

"Like what?" asked Ellen.

"My daddy smokes cigarettes," said Gary. "But he told me he'd spank me if I ever smoked them."

"Maybe your father wishes he didn't smoke," said Ellen. "I bet he doesn't want you to start smoking because he knows it's bad for your health."

"Mom says I should never tell a lie," said Gary. "But when someone on the phone asked to talk to daddy, she said he wasn't home—but he was."

"Sometimes adults do things like that," Ellen said.

"Do you think it's right?" asked Gary.

"No," said Ellen. "But they make mistakes too. Just like kids do."

"But they shouldn't think that they can do things we can't do," Gary said.

"But there are some things adults can do that kids shouldn't do," Ellen said.

"Like what?" asked Gary.

"They can drive cars," said Ellen. "I'm taking lessons now. They can get married. They can write checks."

"OK," said Gary, "they can do some things kids can't do. But adults should listen to what they tell us to do. And they should do the same thing."

Some questions

Do you think God has given different rules to adults than to children?

Do adults and children both have to be forgiven?

Why do children have to wait until they are adults to do some things?

A prayer

Dear God, help us children to understand adults, and help us adults to understand children. And help all of us to forgive each other when we are wrong. In Jesus' name. Amen.

That's Not My Job
Philippians 2:5-8

"Jackie," her mother called, "will you go and get the dirty clothes out of the basket?"

"I'm busy!" said Jackie.

"So am I," said her mother. "That's why I asked you."

"That's not my job!" said Jackie.

"Since I told you to do it, it *is* your job," said her mother. "You get those clothes. We'll talk about it later."

Jackie went to get the clothes.

That night Jackie was playing with her cat when her mother came and sat down beside her.

"I was in a big hurry this morning and didn't have time to talk about something important," her mother said. "Can we talk about it now?"

"I guess so," said Jackie.

"Remember when I asked you to do something and you said it wasn't your job?" said her mother.

"Yes," Jackie said.

"What do you think your jobs are?" asked her mother.

"I set the table and I make my own bed," said Jackie.

"That's right," said her mother. "And you do those jobs well. Is that all?"

"I think so," Jackie said.

"What do you think my job is?" her mother asked.

"You go to work," said Jackie. "You cook and clean house."

"That's right," said her mother. "But maybe there's a better way for each of us to look at our jobs. Maybe my job is to help you and your job is to help me."

"I *do* help you," Jackie said.

"I know that, and I appreciate what you do," her mother said. "But if *you* only do certain jobs and *I* only do certain jobs, some things won't get done. We are a family. Some things have to be done that aren't on anyone's list. That's when we have to help each other."

"OK," said Jackie, "I'll try."

"Fine!" said her mother. "Let's think of working and playing together as a family as our real job."

Some questions

Who divides up the jobs in your family?

Do you do only what you have to do or do you do what has to be done?

How can you help others in your family? How can others help you?

A prayer

Thank you, God, for our family. Help us to live together happily by helping each other. In Jesus' name. Amen.

Something to Give
Luke 21:1-4

"Are you ready for church?" Clark's mother asked him.

"As soon as I tie my shoes," said Clark, who wanted everyone in the family to know he could do it himself.

"Do you have your money for the offering?" his mother asked.

"No," Clark said. "Will you give me some?"

"I gave you your allowance yesterday," said his mother. "You know you are to use part of it for your offering."

"But I spent it all at the school picnic," said Clark.

"You should have taken out your offering for God before you went to the picnic," his mother said.

"I only give 50 cents anyway," Clark said. "It won't make any difference if I miss this Sunday."

"The amount you give is not as important as why you give it," said his mother. "Giving shows that God is important in your life."

"God's important to me. But so was the school picnic."

"We want you to enjoy the picnic and other things," his mother said. "But we also want you to plan how you spend your money. If you take your offering out of your allowance first, you will be making God a part of all that you do."

"Is God a part of the school picnic?" asked Clark.

"Of course!" said his mother. "Jesus is with us all the time. He wants us to enjoy life."

"Then why are you talking to me about what I give at church?" Clark asked.

"Because you need to learn how to give if you are going to enjoy life," his mother said. "Those who always put themselves first do not enjoy life."

"But I don't have anything to give today!" said Clark.

"Then I will lend you 50 cents," said his mother. "Next Saturday you will get 50 cents less."

Some questions

What part of your money do you use to help others?
Do you enjoy giving to God when you worship?
Does even the small amount given by a child help the church?

A prayer

Thank you, God, for the money I have. Help me to spend it, give it, and save it in the right way. In Jesus' name. Amen.

Jesus Loves Us All
John 17:20

Tania and her parents were driving to church on Sunday morning. They passed another church on the way.

"Why can't we go to that church?" Tania asked her parents.

"It may be a fine church," said her mother, "but we go to our church."

"My friend Karen goes to that church," said Tania. "She asked me to go to church with her."

"That's fine!" said her father. "If you want to, you can go some Sunday."

"No, she wants me to go there all the time," Tania said. "She says I can't go to heaven unless I go to that church."

"I'm afraid Karen hasn't gotten things straight or hasn't been taught right," her father said. "Has your Sunday school teacher told you how you can go to heaven?"

"Yes," said Tania.

"Is heaven only for people who go to our church?" he asked.

"No," Tania said. "My teacher said heaven is for everyone who believes in Jesus, and that Jesus wants all of us to be with him."

"Your Sunday school teacher is right," said her mother.

"Then why do we have different churches?" asked Tania.

"Some churches teach one thing and some teach another," her mother said. "But I hope that all churches teach that Jesus' love is for everyone."

"Is our church better than other churches?" Tania asked.

"We like our church," said her father. "But we like it because it teaches us to love everyone like Jesus does. Since Jesus loves everyone, we can love them too."

"What if some people don't love Jesus?" Tania asked.

"Jesus still loves them," said her mother. "And we can help people to love Jesus by loving them too."

"You sound just like my Sunday school teacher!" said Tania.

Some questions

Do you know people who love Jesus and who go to a church that is different from yours?

Do your friends know what church you go to?

Do your friends know that you love Jesus?

A prayer

Dear God, help all people to love each other just like Jesus loves us. Amen.

Your Mother Is Mean
Romans 3:22-24

Shane was glad that he had been able to invite his best friend Rick along on a family camping trip. One night when Shane and Rick could not sleep, they sneaked out of the cabin very quietly and went down to the lake. They sat in a boat and talked.

Later they heard Shane's mother calling their names. They tried to sneak back to the cabin, but she saw them. Shane's mother was angry at them and told them they could not go fishing the next day. She sent them back to bed.

"Boy, your mother is as mean as a 200-year-old weasel," said Rick.

"My mother isn't 200 years old!" said Shane.

"But she's mean," Rick said. "She won't let us go fishing tomorrow."

"How mean is a weasel?" Shane asked.

"I saw one on a nature show once," said Rick. "It was so mean it chased a fox away, and the fox was a lot bigger than the weasel."

"How did it chase the fox?" asked Shane.

"It just got mean and bad," Rick said. "You should have seen those teeth!"

"Why was it so mean?" Shane asked.

"The fox had found its babies and was going to eat them," said Rick. "And that mother weasel chased the fox away."

"Maybe all mothers are mean," said Shane. "Even animals."

"I guess the weasel was mean because she wanted to protect her babies," Rick said.

"Do you think my mother was mean because she wanted to protect us?" asked Shane.

"We're not babies!" said Rick.

"Yeah, but she thinks she's got to watch over us all the time," Shane said.

236

"She probably thought we'd drown or something," Rick said.
"Or maybe she thought someone would kidnap us," said Shane.

"I guess that weasel was right when she chased that fox," said Rick.

"And maybe Mom was mean for a good reason," said Shane.

Some questions

Why do parents want to protect their children?

Do parents always know exactly how to do the right thing?

How can the adults and children in your family do better at helping each other?

A prayer

Dear God, thank you for loving us and helping us. Help us to love and understand one another. In Jesus' name. Amen.

Who Will Take Care of Me?
John 14:18-20

Sara went along with her father when he took the car to a garage to have it fixed. On the way they passed a cemetery.

"When you die, will they put your name on a stone?" Sara asked her father.

"Probably," said her father.

"I'll make sure they spell your name right," said Sara.

"I'd appreciate that," her father said.

"If you and Mom both die, who will take care of me and Sean?" Sara asked. Sean was her baby brother.

"Uncle Art and Aunt Gloria would take care of you."

"Why couldn't we live with Grandpa and Grandma?" asked Sara.

"Your grandparents are getting old," her father said. "Uncle Art and Aunt Gloria could take better care of you."

"Do they know about this?" Sara asked.

"Yes," said her father. "Your mother and I have talked to them about it. We put their names in our will as the people who should take care of you if we both died."

"What's a will?" asked Sara.

"A will is a legal paper we made with a lawyer," her father said. "It tells what to do with our things after we die. In our will we also left instructions for Uncle Art and Aunt Gloria to take care of you."

"Why did you do that?" Sara asked.

"Because we didn't want you to worry about what would happen to you if we died," said her father. "We like to take good care of you."

"I hope you and Mom don't die," said Sara. "But if you do I know you will go to heaven to be with Jesus."

"That's right, Sara!" her father said. "Jesus will take care of us. The will takes care of everything else. So we don't have anything to worry about."

"That's good!" Sara said.

"All I've got to worry about now is getting this car fixed," said her father.

Some questions

Do you know anyone whose mother or father has died?

Who would take care of you if your parents died?

If you have questions about death, whom can you ask for answers?

A prayer

Thank you, Jesus, for my family. Help us to live together happily for a long time; and when we die, take us to heaven to be with you. Amen.

I Don't Know What to Pray For

Romans 8:26-27

"It's time to say your prayers and turn out the light, Scott," his mother said as she came into his room.

"You can turn out the light," he said.

"Have you said your prayers?" his mother asked.

"I'm not going to pray tonight," said Scott.

"Why not?" asked his mother.

"I don't know what to pray for," Scott said.

"What's the problem?" his mother asked.

"If I win at the science show tomorrow, I will get a trip to the big science show next week at the university in the city," said Scott.

"Do you want to pray that you will win?" asked his mother.

"Well, if I win, Chuck will lose," Scott said. "He wants to win because his grandmother lives near the university, and he would get to see her then. And if I win, I will be gone next week and will miss the class picnic."

"Do you want to pray that Chuck will win then?"

"No, I'd like to win," said Scott. "But I also want to go to the picnic. And I want Chuck to see his grandmother."

"I see your problem," said his mother.

"That's why I can't pray," Scott said. "I don't know what to tell God to do."

"Maybe you ought to think a little more about what prayer is," his mother said. "When you pray, you don't tell God what to do; you ask God to help."

"How do I ask God for help when I don't know what I want?" asked Scott.

"Just tell him what you told me," said his mother. "Then ask God to do what is best for you and for Chuck and for everyone else."

"You mean I don't have to tell God what I want?" Scott asked.

"No," his mother said. "When I pray, I often ask God what he wants. God knows how to solve problems that bother us."

"I'm glad he does," said Scott, "because I sure don't!"

Some questions

Are you always sure about what you should pray for?

Can you ask God for help even when you don't know what kind of help you need?

A prayer

Dear God, sometimes I don't know what to say, but I know I want to ask for your help. Will you help me anyway, please? In Jesus' name. Amen.

Act Your Age
2 Peter 3:18

Kurt was spending the weekend with his grandmother. He liked being with her because they could talk about lots of things.

"Grandma," he asked, "do you think I act my age?"

"Yes, Kurt," said his grandmother, "I think you act like a seven-year-old boy should act."

"Dad and Mom don't think so!" he said.

"What makes you think that?" asked his grandmother.

"Dad always tells me to act my age so he must think I don't," said Kurt. "And the other day Mom told me to stop acting like a baby."

"Do you think you were acting like a baby?" his grandmother asked.

"No," he said. "Babies wet their diapers and cry a lot. But I still cry sometimes," he added.

"That's all right," said his grandmother. "Seven-year-olds can cry sometimes. But you cry for different reasons and in a different way than a baby."

"Sometimes Mom and Dad treat me like a baby," said Kurt, "and other times they tell me I'm too old to do the things I want to do. I wish they'd make up their minds!"

"In some ways you are grown-up," his grandmother said. "You are potty-trained, you feed yourself, you dress yourself, and you can read and write. Can you remember when you first started school and couldn't do those things?"

"Sure!" Kurt said, "But now I'm as grown-up as anyone in my class."

"That's true," said his grandmother. "You're doing fine. But you still have a lot more growing to do. Look at your cousin Ted. He is a lot more grown-up—and he should be, because he is 10. Each time you get a year older, you grow up some more because you learn more."

"When will I be finished and all grown-up?" asked Kurt.

"I don't know. I'm only 67 years old and I'm still growing up," his grandmother said. "I'm still learning new things and doing new things. So I'm still changing, and that means I'm still growing up."

"I hope I grow up to be like you, Grandma!" said Kurt.

Some questions

Can you think of some ways that you have grown up in the last year?

How do you want to grow up even more in the next year?

Do you think older people can still act young?

A prayer

Dear God, help me to learn what you have to teach me now, and help me to grow up to be a good and happy person. In Jesus' name. Amen.

She Was Naked

Genesis 1:26-28, 31

"Mom, when my friends come to play, will you make Amy stay out of my room and out of my way?" Brian demanded.

"What's the matter now?" asked his mother.

"I was in my room playing with Mark and Sean," said Brian. "And Amy came in."

"Amy is only two years old," said his mother. "She didn't want to bother you; she just wanted to be with you."

"But she was naked!" Brian said. "She ought to be ashamed."

"She didn't think about putting clothes on," his mother said. "I had just given her a bath and the phone rang before I could get her dressed."

"But she shouldn't run around the house without clothes," said Brian, "—especially when my friends are here."

"I understand how you feel, Brian," said his mother. "But I hope you know that there is nothing wrong with our bodies. God created Amy without any clothes, and she doesn't need to be ashamed of her body."

"I don't want to run around the house naked," Brian said.

"I'm glad you don't," his mother said. "But when you were Amy's age, you sometimes did—and that was all right. As you get older, you learn to be modest about your body—and that's good too."

"I just don't want people looking at me naked," said Brian.

"That's fine!" said his mother. "When you were Amy's age, your father and I used to have you in the bath with us, just as we do with Amy now. But as you got older, we wanted you to have privacy for yourself just like we want privacy for ourselves. I'm glad you know when you should keep your body covered."

"But Mark and Sean giggled when she came in the room," Brian said.

"They may have been embarrassed and didn't know what to say," his mother said. "I wouldn't have let Amy walk in if I had been there. But I don't want anyone to make fun of your body or anyone else's. Our bodies are God's good creation."

Where would it be all right for you to be naked?

Where should you not be naked?

Should you laugh at (or say bad things about) the parts of our bodies that we keep covered?

A prayer

Dear God, thank you for giving us beautiful bodies. Help us to respect and take care of our bodies. In Jesus' name. Amen.

Christmas
Luke 2:1-20

"If Mary and Joseph would have come to our house we would have had room for them," Kyle said after his father had read the story of Jesus' birth from Luke 2.

"I hope so," said his father. "But would we have put them in the garage like the innkeeper put them in the stable?"

"No," said Kyle. "They would have the bed that Grandma uses when she comes to visit us."

"But what if Grandma were here visiting us?" said his mother. "There were many visitors in Bethlehem when Jesus was born."

"Then they could have my room," Kyle said.

"I like that idea!" said his mother.

"And in one way that's what happened," his father said.

"How?" asked Kyle.

"Jesus is in your room," said his father.

"No," said Kyle. "He lived in Bethlehem of Judea. That's the part I said in the Sunday school program."

"That's where Jesus lived then," his father said. "But now he lives in all of us who believe in him. When you go to bed in your room, you pray to him. Do you think he hears you?"

"Of course!" Kyle said.

"Is he there with you?" asked his father.

"He's always with me because he loves me," said Kyle. He remembered that from the Sunday school program too.

"That's why the Christmas story is such a happy story for us," said his father. "It tells us that God wants to be with us."

"And God even lived in a stable for us," said Kyle.

"Yes," his mother said. "But the stable is not the important part. Jesus came to be our Savior so that he can be with us always. Now he can be with us wherever we are."

"Like when we ride in the car," Kyle said.

"He's also in the hospital with people who are ill," said his father.

"And in school with you," his mother said.

"And Jesus is with us when we open our presents right now," said Kyle.

Some questions

Where is it easy for you to know Jesus is with you?
Where is it difficult for you to know Jesus is with you?
How can Christmas help you know Jesus is with you?

A prayer

Jesus, thank you for coming to live with us and to save us. Please be with us always. Amen.

Good Friday
Matthew 27:45-56

"Why was there a big black cloth over the cross?" Karen asked her parents on the way home from church on Good Friday.

"Because this is the day Jesus died," said her sister Sharon.

"That's right," said their mother. "We use black cloth as a sign of sadness. People used to wear only black clothes after someone in their family died."

"But if it's a sad day, why do we call it 'Good Friday'?" asked Karen.

"It *is* a good day, the best day of all," said her mother. "Jesus died for us because he loves us."

"But you don't have to die because you love someone," Sharon said.

"That's true most of the time," said her mother. "I love you, but I probably won't have to die for you."

"Then why did Jesus have to die?" asked Sharon.

"Jesus died to take away our sins," her mother said. "We call that a sacrifice. He took our place."

"You mean we should die because of our sins?" asked Karen.

"Yes," said her mother. "That's why we are sad today. We know that it was because of us that Jesus had to die."

"But if Jesus had to die for us, why is this a good day?" Karen asked.

"Because our happiness is bigger than our sadness," her mother said. "We are sad because we have sinned. But we are happy that Jesus loves us and took our sin away."

"Did we make Jesus die?" asked Sharon.

"No," said her mother, "he died because he loved us. Jesus wants to be our Savior. He wants us to live with him forever."

"Could we put a black cloth on our cross at home?" asked Karen.

"I think that would be a good idea," her mother said. "But remember, the sadness is only for a little while. On Sunday we will celebrate because that's the day God brought Jesus back to life."

Some questions

Can you be happy even on the day Jesus died?
Can you be happy even when someone you love dies?
What makes this a good day for you?

A prayer

Thank you for loving us so much, Jesus. We love you. Help us to see your love for all people so that we may love them too. Amen.

Easter

John 20:1-9

"We have another surprise for you this morning," said Mr. Boyd as the family drove away from church on Easter morning.

"What is it?" asked Matt.

"Do we get to eat our Easter eggs now?" asked Laura.

"Easter is a happy day for us," said their mother, "so we are going to a nice restaurant for brunch."

"What's brunch?" Laura asked.

"That's breakfast and lunch together," said their mother.

When the Boyd family went into the restaurant they were seated at a small table. Most of the other people were in large groups and sat at big tables.

"Why are there so many people here?" asked Matt.

"Some of them are celebrating because their families are all together today. Others might be celebrating other things. We are here to celebrate too."

"What are we celebrating?" asked Laura.

"Think about what we heard at church today," said her mother. "We really have something to be happy about."

"Because Jesus was dead and now he is alive again?" said Laura.

"Right!" her mother said.

Matt and Laura enjoyed watching all the people. About 25 people sat at one table. They listened as a man said, "Congratulations to John and Cora on their 50th wedding anniversary." Everyone at the table cheered.

There were a lot of young people at another table. They sang "Happy Birthday" to someone named Ronnie.

Then it became more quiet in the restaurant because everyone was eating. Then Matt had an idea.

"I just want to say," Matt said in a loud voice, "that I'm glad Jesus is alive!"

Some questions

How does your family celebrate a happy event?
What makes you happy at Easter?
How can you share your joy with others?

A prayer

Lord Jesus, thank you for Easter and for being with us today. We are happy as we celebrate your victory over death. Amen.

Pentecost
Acts 2:1-12

Adam was happy because his friend Joel was spending the weekend with him. On Saturday night Adam's mother helped them get ready for bed. She turned out the light and told them to go to sleep.

"Why do you have to go to bed so early on Saturday night?" asked Joel. "I always stay up late, because I can sleep as long as I like on Sunday."

"We get up and go to church and Sunday school on Sunday," said Adam. "I hope you will come along with me tomorrow."

"What do you do at church?" Joel asked.

"Lots of things," Adam said.

"Like what?" asked his friend.

"My Sunday school teacher said we would be doing something special tomorrow because it's Pentecost," said Adam.

"What's Pentecost?" Joel asked.

"My teacher says that's the day the Holy Spirit came," Adam said.

"You believe in spirits?" asked Joel.

"Not spirits," said Adam. "The *Holy* Spirit!"

"Who's that?" Joel asked.

"That's another name for God," Adam said. "We're going to do a play about the Holy Spirit in Sunday school tomorrow. I'm going to be one of the disciples. You'll be able to see it."

"What are you going to do?" asked Joel.

"First the teacher will turn on a fan so that we can hear a wind," said Adam. "Then we'll put a piece of fire on our heads."

"Real fire?" Joel asked.

"No," Adam said. "It's only red paper. But it reminds us how the Holy Spirit came so that people could tell other people about Jesus."

"I'd like to go with you to Sunday school tomorrow and see your play," said Joel.

"Great!" said Adam.

Some questions

What are some stories about Jesus that you remember?

Can you talk to other people about Jesus?

How can the Holy Spirit help you listen to others who tell you about Jesus?

Are there things that the Holy Spirit would like you to do that will help you learn more about Jesus?

A prayer

Dear God, thank you for the Holy Spirit, who teaches us. Help me to teach others about Jesus. Amen.

Prayers

General

Thank you, Jesus
for being here.
Help me know
you're always near.
Amen.

Thank you, God,
for moms and dads,
for girls and boys,
for chairs and beds,
for games and toys,
for dogs and cats,
for church and school,
for balls and bats,
for books and pencils,
for houses and cars,
for night and day,
for sun and stars,
for food and clothes.
Amen.

Dear Jesus,
help me help others.
Help others help me.
Amen.

Dear Jesus,
I need to talk to you —
but not very much.
I just have to say:
help me, thank you,
and such.
Amen.

Dear God,
Sometimes I think
no one loves me.
Please love me so much
that I can love others;
and they can love me too.
In Jesus' name. Amen.

Morning

Good morning, God.
It's a new day.
Show me how
to go your way.
Amen.

Evening

Thank you, God,
for the blessings of this day:
    for the food I ate,
    for my family and friends,
    for the fun I had,
    for the help you gave,
and for the other things
I can't remember right now.
In Jesus' name. Amen.

Good night, Jesus,
thanks for today.
While I am asleep,
don't go away.
Amen.

Mealtime

Thank you, God,
for this food,
and for those
who cooked it.
For these dishes,
and for those who
will wash them.
For those who eat here,
and for Jesus
who loves us all.
Amen.

Come, Lord Jesus,
sit at our table.
Bless us as we eat
and keep us able.
Amen.

Lord,
bless this food,
those who grew it,
those who cooked it,
and those who eat it.
Amen.

Birthday

Dear God,
Bless _____ on (his/her) birthday.
Thank you for giving (him/her) to us.
And thank you for giving us to (him/her).
In Jesus' name. Amen.

For Health

When I am hurting,
and when I am ill,
be with me, Jesus,
and make me well.
Amen.

Dear God,
please make _____ well.
In Jesus' name. Amen.

For Family

Thank you, God,
for my father
and my mother
and all the others
who add love to my life.
Help me add love
to their lives.
In Jesus' name. Amen.

Dear Lord,
bless our family.
Love us all.
Keep us together.
Don't let us fall.
Amen.

Dear God,
Thanks for our home
for its furniture and rooms,
for the fun we have,
for the flower that blooms.
Amen.

Before a Trip

Come with us, Jesus,
we're going for a drive.
Give us a safe trip.
Make us happy
when we arrive.
Amen.

Dear Jesus,
Bless our car
when we ride.
Keep us safe,
be at our side.
Amen.

School

Dear Jesus,
come with me
to school today.
Help me in all I do
and say.
Help me do right.
Don't let me fight.
For all your blessings
I pray.
Amen.

God bless my teacher.
God bless my friends.
God bless our school,
and each who attends.
Amen.

Index